ST. THOMAS AQUINAS
COMMENTARY ON COLOSSIANS

ST. THOMAS AQUINAS
COMMENTARY ON COLOSSIANS

COMMENTARY BY ST. THOMAS AQUINAS

ON THE EPISTLE TO THE COLOSSIANS

TRANSLATED BY FABIAN LARCHER, OP

EDITED BY DANIEL A. KEATING

Requests for permission to make copies of any part of the work should
be directed to:

Sapientia Press
of Ave Maria University
1025 Commons Circle
Naples, Florida 34119
888-343-8607

Cover Design: Eloise Anagnost

Printed in the United States of America.

Library of Congress Control Number: 2006928346

ISBN-10: 1-932589-32-5
ISBN-13: 978-1-932589-32-0

Table of Contents

Acknowledgments

IN COLLABORATION with Sapientia Press, the Aquinas Center for Theological Renewal is pleased to publish this translation of St. Thomas Aquinas's *Lectura super Epistolam ad Colossenses*. At his death, Fabian Larcher, OP, left in the care of his confrere Pierre Conway, OP (who has also recently passed to the Lord), a nearly complete set of translations of Aquinas's commentaries on the epistles of St. Paul. But few of these translations have appeared in print, due both to the unedited state in which most of Father Larcher's translations were left, and to the fact that the translations were not based on critical editions of the texts of the original commentaries. To further complicate matters and delay publication of Father Larcher's work, there is the fact that Aquinas's commentaries on St. Paul were not directly composed by Aquinas. Instead they are scribes' notes of Aquinas's lectures, and revised only lightly—and in the case of Colossians probably not at all—by Aquinas himself. Yet, Aquinas did approve the publication of the entire collection of his commentaries on Paul and he wrote a preface to them, so there can be no question about including them among his works.

Daniel A. Keating of Sacred Heart Major Seminary carefully read through Father Larcher's translation of Aquinas's commentary on Colossians, typed it, and corrected it to accord with the Marietti edition of the text, including the addition of the Marietti paragraph numbers. While Professor Keating would be the first to say that it is still by no means a critical edition, all who seek to learn from St. Thomas Aquinas now find themselves much in Professor Keating's debt. Without his work, this publication would not have been possible. The deepest thanks are due to Fathers Larcher and Conway. In numerous letters and conversations before his death, Father Conway strongly urged the publication of this text and of the remaining unpublished translations undertaken by Father Larcher. We are profoundly grateful to him for his encouragement.

Lastly, we owe a significant debt of gratitude to Ave Maria University, which generously provided us with the research funding that made possible the publication of the volume.

—Michael Dauphinais and Matthew Levering
Co-Directors, Aquinas Center for Theological Renewal
Feast of Saint Catherine of Siena, 2006

Prologue

"HE protected the camp with his sword."
—1 MACC 3:3

---

1   This passage is appropriate to the subject matter of this letter to the Colossians, because this present life is a battle waged by soldiers who live in a camp: "The life of man on earth is a war" (JOB 7:1). And so the place where the faithful live is called a camp. And the Church is like a camp: "This is the camp of God" (GEN 32:2).

This camp is attacked in three ways. First, by those aggressors who openly rise against the Church: "They marched up over the broad earth and surrounded the camp of the saints and the beloved city" (REV 20:9). Second, this camp is deceitfully undermined by heretics: "By fair and flattering words they deceive the hearts of the simpleminded" (ROM 16:18); "Evil men and imposters; will go from bad to worse, deceivers and deceived" (2 TIM 3:13). Third, it is attacked by some of its own members who have become depraved from sins that spring from the corruption of the flesh: "The desires of the flesh are against the Spirit, and the desires of the Spirit are against the flesh" as we read in Galatians (5:17); "For we are not contending against flesh and blood, but against the principalities, against the powers, against the world rulers of this present darkness" (EPH 6:12).

In this war the prelates of the Church are our leaders: according to the Psalm "The princes of Judah are their leaders" (PS 68:27). It is their duty to protect the camp of the Church against all these attacks. First, against sins, by encouraging the people: "Declare to my people their transgression, to the house of Jacob their sins" (IS 58:1). Second, against heretics, by their sound teaching: "He must hold firm to the sure word as taught, so that he may be able to give instruction in sound doctrine and also to confute those who contradict it" (TIT 1:9). Third, they should protect the Church against those who persecute it by giving an example of patient suffering.

This is the way Paul protected the Church with his spiritual sword, because in his letters he combated sin, refuted heresies, and encouraged patience. As to the first: "But immorality and all impurity or covetousness must not even be named among you, as is fitting among saints" (EPH 5:3). As to the second: "As for a man that is factious, after admonishing him once or twice, have nothing more to do with him" (TIT 3:10). As to the third, the entire eleventh chapter of his second letter to the Corinthians shows how he encouraged them to be patient.

2 The passage quoted at the beginning mentions two of these matters: the condition of the Church, when it says, **camp**, and the zeal of the Apostle, when it says **protected**.

Now a camp has to be alert in order to avoid evil: "Your camp must be holy" (DT 23:14); and it should have a good relationship with its leader and in itself: "This is the camp of God" (GEN 32:21). It should also be a threat to the enemy: "Terrible as an army with banners" (SG 6:10).

Now the Apostle was alert in protecting them, like a shepherd, whose duty is to carefully lead his sheep so they are not lost. "He goes before them, and the sheep follow him" (JN 10:4). The Apostle did act this way: "Be imitators of me, as I am of Christ" (1 COR 4:16). A shepherd should also feed his flock generously, so they do not become ill: "Tend the flock of God that is your charge" (1 PET 5:2). And the Apostle did this also: "I fed you with milk" (1 COR 3:2).

A shepherd should also bravely defend his flock, so they will not be destroyed: "Do not seek to become a judge, lest you be unable to remove iniquity" (SIR 7:6); "Your servant used to keep sheep for his father; and when there came a lion or a bear, and took a lamb from the flock, I went after him and delivered it out of his mouth" (1 SAM 17:34). And so our beginning text says that the Apostle **protected the camp**, that is, God's Church, **with a sword**, which is the word of God: "The word of God is living and active, sharper then any two-edged sword" (HEB 4:12).

Here, then, is the subject matter of this letter. In his letter to the Ephesians, the Apostle described the nature of the Church's unity; and in the letter to the Philippians, he showed its growth and preservation. But in this letter he is dealing with its protection from those heretics who were corrupting and misleading the Colossians.

Chapter 1 ▪ Lectura 1

COLOSSIANS 1:1–2

---

¹**PAUL, an apostle of Christ Jesus by the will of God, and Timothy our brother, ²To the saints and faithful brethren in Christ at Colossae: Grace to you and peace from God our Father.**

---

3 This letter is divided into its greeting and its message (1:3). First, the persons sending the letter are mentioned; then, the ones to whom it is sent (1:2); and third, the good things desired for the latter (1:2B). As to the first, the principal sender is mentioned, and second, his companion.

4 The principal sender of this letter is first identified by his name, **Paul**, that is, one who is humble, for it is such persons who receive wisdom: "You have hidden these things from the wise and understanding and revealed them to babes" (MT 11:25), and so Paul can teach this wisdom.

Second, the sender is described by his office, namely, **an apostle**, that is, one who is sent, to bring salvation to the faithful: "Set apart for me Saul and Barnabas for the work to which I have called them" (ACTS 13:2); "As the Father has sent me, even so I send you" (JN 20:21). He is not the apostle of just anyone, but **of Christ Jesus**, whose glory he seeks, and not his own: "For what we preach is not ourselves, but Jesus Christ as Lord, with ourselves as your servants for Jesus' sake" (2 COR 4:5).

But at times some reach their office because God is angered by a people's sins: "Who makes a man who is a hypocrite to reign for the sins of the people" (JOB 34:30); "I have given you kings in my anger" (HOS 13:11). And so Paul says that he has his office **by the will of God**, that is, by his pleasure: "I will give you shepherds after my own heart, who will feed you with knowledge and understanding" (JER 3:15).

5   The other person to send this letter is **Timothy, our brother**, so that there may be two or three witnesses, as in Deuteronomy (17:6). "A brother helped is like a strong city" (PR 18:19).

6   The persons to whom this letter is sent are **the saints and faithful brethren at Colossae**. The greater ones are called saints: "Let us serve him in holiness and righteousness" (LK 1:74); and the lesser ones are referred to as the **faithful**, who have at least kept the true faith, because "without faith it is impossible to please God" (HEB 11:6). Or we could say, to the saints, that is, to those sanctified by baptism, **and faithful brethren**, that is, those who have remained in the faith they accepted: "A faithful man will be much praised," as we read in Proverbs (28:20).

7   Then he mentions the good things he wishes them to have: that is, **grace**, which is the source of every good: "Justified by his grace as a gift" (ROM 3:24); and **peace**, which is the last of all goods: "He makes peace in your borders" (PS 147:14). As a consequence, he wishes them all the goods that lie between these two. "The Lord will give grace and glory" (PS 84:11). From the **Father** of our Lord Jesus Christ, that is, the Father of Christ by nature, and our Father by grace; **and from the Lord Jesus Christ** [Vulgate]. And so, **from our Father**, that is, God in his Trinity, **and from the Lord Jesus Christ**, considering the nature God assumed.

Chapter 1 ▪ Lectura 2

COLOSSIANS 1:3–8

▪
---

³**WE always thank God, the Father of our Lord Jesus Christ, when we pray for you, ⁴because we have heard of your faith in Christ Jesus and of the love which you have for all the saints, ⁵because of the hope laid up for you in heaven. Of this you have heard before in the word of the truth, the gospel ⁶which has come to you, as indeed in the whole world it is bearing fruit and growing—so among yourselves, from the day you heard and understood the grace of God in truth, ⁷as you learned it from Epaphras our beloved fellow servant. He is a faithful minister of Christ on your behalf ⁸and has made known to us your love in the Spirit.**

▪
---

8 Here Paul begins his message. First, he commends the truth of the Gospel; second, he defends this against those who attack it (in the second chapter). In regard to the first he does two things. First, he commends the truth of faith in the Gospel; and second, its Author (1:15). The first is divided into two parts. First, he thanks God for the benefits conferred on the Colossians in particular; and second, for those benefits granted to the Church in general (1:12). In regard to the first he does two things. First, he thanks God, and second, he shows why he gives thanks (1.14). Again the first is divided into two parts. First, he gives thanks; second, he prays (13b).

9 So he says, **We thank God**, the Author of grace: "Give thanks in all circumstances" (1 TH 5:18). And we thank God **always**, for the past and for the future. For although we cannot actually pray every minute, we should always pray by serving God out of love: "Pray constantly" (1 TH 5:17); "We ought always to pray" (LK 18:1).

10 Then he states his reasons for giving thanks. First, he recalls the blessings they have; and second, how they were obtained (1:5b).

11 Our blessings or goods consist especially in faith, hope, and the love of charity: for by faith we have a knowledge of God; by hope we are raised up to him; but by the love of charity we are united to him. As we read: "So faith, hope, love, abide, these three; but the greatest of these is love" (1 COR 13:13). So he gives thanks for these three. First, that they have the faith; although he was not the one who preached to them, but rather a disciple by the name of Epaphras, and later Archippus. Thus he says, **we have heard of your faith**, which is the beginning of the spiritual life: "The righteous shall live by his faith" (HAB 2:4); "For whoever would draw near to God must believe that he exists and that he rewards those who seek him" (HEB 11:6).

But this faith is dead without an active love, as James says (2:26), and so an active love must also be present: "For in Christ Jesus neither circumcision counts for anything, nor uncircumcision, but a new creation" (GAL 6:15). And so he continues, **and of the love which you have for all the saints**.

There is a love that springs from charity, and another that is worldly. This worldly love does not include everyone, because we love those with whom there is some communication or sharing, which is the cause of love; but in worldly love this cause is not present in everyone, but is only found in one's relatives or other worldly people. But the love of charity does extend to everyone, and, so he says, **for all**. For even though sinners are loved by the love of charity, it is in order that at some time they become holy: "We know that we have passed out of death into life, because we love the brethren" (1 JN 3:14).

Further, the fruit of worldly love is obtained in this world; but the fruit of the love of charity is in eternal life. This leads him to mention hope: **because of the hope laid up for you in heaven**, that is, because of your eternal glory, which is called hope because it is considered as certain: "This hope has been put in my heart," as we read in Job (19:27) [Vulgate].

12   Then (1:5b), he shows how they obtained these things. First, he commends the doctrine of the Gospel; and second, its ministry. First he commends the truth of the doctrine; second, its growth (v. 6); third, its fruitful progress (v. 6b).

13   So he says, **of this you have heard**, that is, of the hope or else of the things hoped for, **in the word of the truth**, the Gospel, for this is greater than everything else: "Eye has not seen, nor ear heard, nor the heart of man conceived what God has prepared for those who love him" (1 COR 2:9). Therefore, God revealed this: "Repent, for the kingdom of heaven is at hand" (MT 3:2). But his hope is true, and not a vain hope (as when the one promising is a liar), because it is **in the word of the truth**: "Your word is truth" (JN 17:17).

14   Then when he says, **which has come to you**, Christ's doctrine is commended for its growth, because it has come not only to you, but is **indeed in the whole world**: "Their voice goes out through all the earth, and their words to the end of the world" (PS 19:4); "This Gospel of the kingdom will be preached throughout the whole world . . . and then the end will come" (MT 24:14).

But since the Gospel has been preached in the whole world, why has the end not come? I answer that some say that the Gospel of Christ is not the Gospel of the kingdom. But this is false, because our Lord calls it the Gospel of the kingdom. And so, according to Chrysostom, we should say that while the apostles were still alive, the Gospel of Christ was throughout the whole world, at least by some kind of report. And it is quite miraculous that Christ's doctrine should have grown so much in forty years. And so the Apostle says, **in the whole world**, that is, by report; and "then the end will come," that is, the destruction of Jerusalem.

But Augustine does not agree with this interpretation, because even in his own time there were some countries in which there were yet no churches. So he says the time referred to is the time when the Gospel will be really preached. Thus the end will come after the Church has become established in all countries, even though some people are not believers. And this end is not at the time of the Apostle, but concerns the end of the world. And so when Paul says here, **in the whole world**, he is speaking of the future; but he is using the present tense because the outcome is so certain. Yet we can say that the Gospel is in the whole world by report, although it is not actually established in all places.

15   Then he commends Christ's doctrine because of its fruit in good works: **It is bearing fruit**: "My blossoms became glorious and abundant fruit" (SIR 24:17); "He indeed bears fruit, and yields, in one case a hundredfold, in another sixty, and in another thirty" (MT 13:23), **and** it is **growing**, that is, in the number of its believers: "The Lord added to their number day by day those who were being saved" (ACTS 2:47). This was the effect of a great power, because as **among yourselves**, so also among others. **From the day you heard**, that is, the preaching, **and understood**, you accepted it.

16   Then he commends its ministry: first, in relation to himself; then in relation to them; and finally in relation to both. So he says, You have been taught the Gospel, **as you learned it from Epaphras, our beloved fellow servant**: "I am a fellow servant with you and your brethren the prophets" (REV 22:9). **He is a faithful minister**, that is, one who does not seek his own profit: "This is how one should regard us, as servants of Christ and stewards of the mysteries of God. Moreover, it is required of stewards that they be found trustworthy" (1 COR 4:1). **He is a faithful minister**, that is, a mediator between them and the Apostle, **and has made known**, that is, indicated, **to us your love in the Spirit**.

Chapter 1 ▪ Lectura 3

COLOSSIANS 1:9–14

▪

⁹**AND** so, from the day we heard of it, we have not ceased to pray for you, asking that you may be filled with the knowledge of his will in all spiritual wisdom and understanding, ¹⁰to lead a life worthy of the Lord, fully pleasing to him, bearing fruit in every good work and increasing in the knowledge of God. ¹¹May you be strengthened with all power, according to his glorious might, for all endurance and patience with joy, ¹²giving thanks to the Father, who has qualified us to share in the inheritance of the saints in light. ¹³He has delivered us from the dominion of darkness and transferred us to the kingdom of his beloved Son, ¹⁴in whom we have redemption, the forgiveness of sins.

▪

17 Above, the Apostle gave the reason for his thanksgiving by mentioning the things for which he gave thanks; here he states his prayer, showing what he is asking for them. First, he gives the characteristics of prayer; second, he mentions the goods he is asking for (v. 9b).

18 Prayer has three characteristics. First, it is timely, thus he says, **from the day we heard of it** we began to pray: "Since I spoke of him, I will still remember him" (JER 31:20).

Second, it is continuous: **We have not ceased to pray for you**: "Far be it from me that I should sin against the Lord by ceasing to pray for you" (1 SAM 12:23); "Without ceasing I mention you always in my prayers" (ROM 1:9).

Third, prayer has several elements and is complete: **to pray for . . . asking**. Praying is lifting our minds up to God; and asking is requesting things. Praying should come first, so that the one devoutly requesting is heard, just as those who are requesting something begin by trying to persuade their listener and bend him to their wishes. But we should begin with devotion and meditation on God and divine things, not in order to bend him, but to lift ourselves up to him.

19 He asks for three things. First, for a knowledge of the truth; second, that they act in a virtuous way (V. 10); and third, that they have the endurance to stand up under evil (V. 11b).

20 He requests three kinds of knowledge for them. First, a knowledge of what they are to do; and so he says, **that you may be filled with the knowledge of his will**, that is, that you may fully know the will of God: "This is the will of God, your sanctification," as we read in 1 Thessalonians (4:3). Thus, one who lives in a holy way knows God's will; but one who sins does not know the will of God, because every sinner is ignorant: "That you may prove what is the good and acceptable and perfect will of God" (ROM 12:2).

Second, he wants them to have a knowledge of divine things, **in all wisdom**, which consists in the knowledge of divine things, as Augustine says, "Think of the Lord with uprightness" (WIS 1:1).

Third, he wants them to have an **understanding of spiritual things**, that is, not of these earthly material things: "Now we have received not the spirit of this world, but the Spirit which is from God," as 1 Corinthians (2:12) says. He appropriately associates wisdom and understanding, because wisdom is weak when there is no understanding, as Gregory says, and understanding is useless without wisdom: for wisdom judges and understanding apprehends, and one cannot apprehend without judging, and vice versa. The Gloss says that the first kind of knowledge is taken in general, the second pertains to the active life, and the third to the contemplative life.

21 Further, knowledge by itself is not enough, because "Whoever knows what is right to do and fails to do it, for him it is sin" (JAS 4:17). And therefore, it is necessary to act according to virtue. He touches on this when he says, **to lead a life worthy of the Lord**, for one lives unworthily if he does not live as is fitting for a son of God to live: "As servants of God we commend ourselves in every way: through great endurance, in afflictions, hardships . . ." (2 COR 6:4); "As we solemnly forewarned you" (1 TH 4:6). Second, he touches on a correct intention: **fully pleasing**: "There was one who pleased God and was loved by him" (WIS 4:10). Third, he brings in the desire to make progress, **bearing fruit in every good work**, for one should always try for a further good: "My blossoms became glorious and abundant fruit" (SIR 24:17); "The return you get is sanctification and its end eternal life" (ROM 6:22).

And after one has borne fruit, an increase in knowledge follows, **and increasing in the knowledge of God**; for as a result of eagerly accomplishing the commands of God, a person is disposed for knowledge: "I understand more than the aged, because I keep your precepts" (PS 119:100); "Wisdom will not dwell in a body enslaved to sin" (WIS 1:4). He says, **increasing in the knowledge of God**, and not of the world: "She gave him a knowledge of holy things" (WIS 10:10).

22 Then he mentions their standing up under evils, for to live a virtuous life it is not enough just to know and to will; one must also act in spite of opposition: and this cannot be done without a patient endurance of evils. And so he says, **may you be strengthened with all power**: "Rich in power" (SIR 44:6). Such power, or virtue, comes from God; and so he says, **according to his glorious might**: "Be strong in the Lord" (EPH 6:10). He says, **glorious might**, that is, Christ's, who is the glory of the Father, because to fall into sin is to fall into darkness: "She is a breath of the power of God, and a pure emanation of the glory of the Almighty" (WIS 7:25).

Then when he says, **for all patience and longsuffering**, he prays that they may stand up under adversity. Some people fail because of the difficulties of their adversities; and they need **patience**: "By your patience you will gain your lives" (LK 21:19). Other people fail because their reward is a long time coming; and so he says, **longsuffering**, which enables a person to wait for what was promised: "If it does not come soon, wait for it; because it will come and not delay" (HAB 2:3); "And thus, with his longsuffering, he obtained what was promised" (HEB 6:15). Yet, although some people do avoid these two vices, they do it with sadness; and since this should not be so he says, **with joy**: "Count it all joy, my brethren, when you meet various trials" (JAS 1:2).

23 Then when he says, **giving thanks to God the Father** [Vulgate], he gives thanks for the favors granted to all of the faithful: first for the gift of grace, and second for the fruit of grace (V. 13).

24 And so he says, We pray for you, **giving thanks to God**, as our Creator, and **the Father**, by adopting us, **who has qualified us to share in the inheritance of the saints in light**. Some people have said that the gifts of grace are given because of a person's merit, and that God gives grace to those who are worthy, and does not give grace to those who are unworthy. But this view is rejected by the Apostle, because whatever worth and grace we have was given to us by God, and so also were the effects of grace. And so Paul says, **who has qualified us to share in the inheritance of the saints in light**: "Not that we are sufficient of ourselves to claim anything as coming from us; our sufficiency is from God" (2 COR 3:5). **To share in the inheritance [lot] of the saints in light**. All men are good in their very nature; consequently, they somehow partake of God. But those who are wicked take pleasure in temporal things as their portion: "This is our portion and this our lot" (WIS 2:9), while those who are holy have God himself as their portion: "The Lord is my portion" (LAM 3:24); "The Lord is my chosen portion" (PS 16:5). And so he says, **who has qualified us to share in the lot of the saints**.

25 He says, **in the lot of the saints**, because there are two ways of apportioning things: Sometimes it is done by choosing, as when one person selects this portion, and another one that portion; and sometimes apportionment is by lot: "The lot puts an end to disputes" (PR 18:18). The saints have their portion not because they chose it: "You did not choose me, but I chose you" (JN 15:16), but because God chose them.

(A lot consists in entrusting something to God's judgment. And there are three types of lot: consultative, divining, and apportioning. The first is not evil when dealing in temporal matters; the second is useless and evil; and the third is sometimes allowed in cases of necessity.) The portion of the saints is the possession of the light: "He dwells in unapproachable light" (1 TIM 6:16); "In his hands he hides the light and commands it to come again" (JOB 36:32), and from it there follows the effect of grace, that is, our transference from darkness to light.

26 First, he mentions this transference; and second, the way in which men are the slaves of sin before they receive grace.

For since sin is a darkness, men [before receiving grace] are in the power of darkness, that is, either of the evil spirits or of sins:

"Against the world rulers of this present darkness" (EPH 6:12), "Even the captives of the mighty shall be taken" (IS 49:25). **He has transferred us to the kingdom of his beloved Son**, that is, that we might be the kingdom of God: "My kingdom is not of this world" (JN 18:36). This happens when we are freed from our sins: "You have made them a kingdom and priests to our God" (REV 5:10). Or literally, we are transferred to this kingdom so that we may obtain eternal life: "The kingdom of heaven is at hand" (MT 3:2). And this is what he says, **the kingdom of his beloved Son.**

27 A more literal translation of this phrase would read: **the kingdom of the Son of his love**. As Augustine says in a Gloss, "love" is sometimes taken to mean the Holy Spirit, who is the love of the Father and the Son. But if "love" were always to mean this Person, then the Son would be the Son of the Holy Spirit. So at other times "love" is understood essentially, to indicate the divine essence. Thus the phrase, **of the Son of his love**, can be taken to mean either "of his beloved Son," or it could mean, "of the Son of his [the Father's] essence."

But is it true to say that the Son is the Son of the essence of the Father? I answer that if the possessive case, "of the essence," is taken to indicate the relationship of an efficient cause, it is false because the essence [of the Father] does not generate nor is it generated. Sometimes the possessive case indicates the possession of a form, as when we say a thing is "of an excellent form," that is, it has an excellent form. And if we understand "of the essence" in this way, then the statement is true, that is, the Son has the essence of the Father: "The Father loves the Son, and has given all things into his hand" (JN 3:35).

28 Then when he says, **in whom we have redemption**, he shows the way we have been transferred. For humanity in sin was held down in two ways: first, as a slave—"Every one who commits sin is a slave to sin" (JN 8:34), and second, as deserving punishment and as turned away from God—"Your iniquities have made a separation between you and your God, and your sins have hid his face from you so that he does not hear" (IS 59:2).

But these two things are taken away by Christ, because, as man, he became a sacrifice for us and redeemed us in his blood; and so Paul says, **in whom we have redemption**: "You were bought with a price" (1 COR 6:20); and from Christ, as God, we have **the forgiveness of sins**, because he took away our debt of punishment.

Chapter 1 ▪ Lectura 4

COLOSSIANS 1:15–17

---

¹⁵**HE is the image of the invisible God, the first-born of all creation, ¹⁶for in him all things were created, in heaven and on earth, visible and invisible, whether thrones or dominions or principalities or authorities— all things were created through him and for him. ¹⁷He is before all things, and in him all things hold together.**

---

29 After Paul recalled for us the universal and special benefits of grace, he now commends the Author of this grace, that is, Christ. And he does this, first, in his relation to God; second, in relation to all of creation (15b); and third, in relation to the Church (v. 18).

30 As to the first, we should note that God is said to be **invisible** because he exceeds the capacity of vision of any created intellect, so that no created intellect, by its natural knowledge, can attain His essence: "Behold, God is great, and we know him not" (JOB 36:26); "He dwells in unapproachable light" (1 TIM 6:16). And therefore, he is seen by the blessed by means of grace, and not by reason of their natural capacity.

Dionysius gives the reason for this: All knowledge terminates at something that exists, that is, at some nature that participates in the act of existence *[esse]*; but God is the very act of existence *[ipsum esse]*, not participating in the act of existence, but participated in;

and thus he is not known. It is of this invisible God that the Son is the image.

31   Let us now see in what way the Son is called the image of God, and why he is said to be invisible. The notion of an image includes three things. First, an image must be a likeness; second, it must be derived or drawn from the thing of which it is a likeness; and third, it must be derived with respect to something that pertains to the species or to a sign of the species. For if two things are alike, but neither is derived from the other, then neither one is the image of the other; thus one egg is not said to be the image of another. And so something is called an image because it imitates.

Further, if there is a likeness between two things, but not according to species or a sign of the species, we do not speak of an image. Thus, a man has many accidents, such as color, size, and so on; but they are not the reason for calling something an image of a man. But if something has the shape or figure of a man, then it can be called an image, because this shape is a sign of the species. Now the Son is like the Father, and the Father is like the Son. But because the Son has this likeness from the Father, and not the Father from the Son, we, properly speaking, say that the Son is the image of the Father, and not conversely, for this likeness is drawn and derived from the Father.

Further, this likeness is according to species, because in divine matters the Son is somehow, although faintly, represented by our mental word. We have a mental word when we actually conceive the form of the thing of which we have knowledge; and then we signify this mental word by an external word. And this mental word we have conceived is a certain likeness, in our mind, of the thing, and it is like it in species. And so the Word of God is called the image of God.

32   As to our second question, we should note that the Arians misunderstood the text: for they thought about the image of God as they did of the images they made of their ancestors, so they could see in these images the loved ones no longer with them (just as we make images of the saints to see in these images those whom we cannot see in reality). And so they said that to be invisible was unique to the Father, and that the first visible reality was the Son, who manifested the goodness of the Father. They were saying that the Father was truly invisible, but the Son was visible, and thus their natures would be different. But the Apostle refutes this when he says, "He reflects the glory of God and bears the very stamp of his nature, upholding the universe by his word of power. When he had made purification for sins, he sat down at the right hand of the Majesty on high" (HEB 1:3). And thus the Son is not only the image of the invisible God, but he himself is invisible like the Father: **He is the image of the invisible God**.

33   Then when he says, **the first-born of all creation**, he commends Christ in relation to creatures. First he does so; and second, he amplifies it (V. 16).

34   We should note, about the first point, that the Arians understood this to mean that Christ is called the first-born because he is the first creature. But this is not the meaning, as will be clear. So we have to understand two things: how this image is generated, and in what way it is the first-born of creatures.

In regard to the first, we should note that things generate in various ways depending on their nature and manner of existence, for men generate in one way and plants in another, and so on for other things. But the nature of God is his existence *[ipsum esse]* and his act of understanding *[intelligere]* and so it is necessary that his generating or intellectual conceiving is the generating or conceiving of his nature. (In us, however, our intellectual conceiving is not the conceiving of our nature, because our nature is not the same as our act of understanding.) Therefore, since this image is a word and concept of an intellect, it is necessary to say that it is the offspring of the nature, so that the one receiving the nature from the other is generated by necessity.

35 Second, we have to understand in what way the Son is called the first-born. God does not know himself and creatures through two different sources; he knows all things in his own essence, as in the first efficient cause. The Son, however, is the intellectual concept or representation of God insofar as he knows himself, and, as a consequence, every creature. Therefore, inasmuch as the Son is begotten, he is seen as a word representing every creature, and he is the principle of every creature. For if he were not begotten in that way, the Word of the Father would be the first-born of the Father only, and not of creatures: "I came forth from the mouth of the Most High, the first-born before every creature" (SIR 24:5) [Vulgate].

36 Then when he says, **in him all things were created**, he explains what he has just said, that is, that the Son is the first-born because he was generated as the principle of creatures; and this with respect to three things. First, with respect to the creation of things; in the second place, with respect to their distinction, **in heaven and on earth**, and third, with respect to their preservation in existence, **and in him all things hold together**.

37 He says that the Son is the first-born of every creature because he is generated or begotten as the principle of every creature. And so he says, **for in him all things were created**.

With respect to this, we should note that the Platonists affirmed the existence of Ideas, and said that each thing came to be by participating in an Idea, like the Idea of man, or an Idea of some other kind. Instead of all these we have one, that is, the Son, the Word of God. For an artisan makes an artifact by making it participate in the form he has conceived within himself, enveloping it, so to say, with external matter; for we say that the artisan makes a house through the form of the thing that he has conceived within himself. This is the way God is said to make all things in his wisdom, because the wisdom of God is related to his created works just as the art of the builder is to the house he has made. Now this form and wisdom is the Word; and thus **in him all things were created**, as in an exemplar: "He spoke and they were made" (GEN 1), because he created all things to come into existence in his eternal Word.

38   With respect to the differences among things, we should note that some, like the Manicheans, were mistaken in thinking that earthly bodies, since they are corruptible, were made by an evil god, while the heavenly bodies, because they are incorruptible, were made by the good God, that is, by the Father of Christ. This was an error, because both types of bodies were created in the same [Word]. And so he says, **in heaven and on earth**. This difference is based on the different parts of corporeal nature. "In the beginning," that is, in the Son, "God created the heavens and the earth" (GEN 1:1).

39   The Platonists also said that God created invisible creatures, that is, the angels, by himself, but created bodily natures by the angels. But this is refuted here, because Paul says, **visible and invisible**. As to the first he says, "By faith we understand that the world was framed by the word of God; that from invisible things visible things might be made" (HEB 11:3). About the second we read, "We have seen but few of his works. For the Lord has made all things, and to the godly he has granted wisdom" (SIR 43:32–33). This difference in things is based on the nature of created things.

40   The third difference is concerned with the order and degrees found in invisible realities, when he says, **whether thrones or**

dominions or principalities or authorities. The Platonists were mistaken in this matter for they said that there are different perfections found in things, and attributed each of these to its own first principle. And they said there was an order of principles according to the orders of these perfections. Thus they affirmed a first being, from whom all things participate in existence; and another principle, distinct from this, a first intellect, from which all things participate in intelligence; and then another principle, life, from which all things participate in life.

But we do not agree with this, for all the perfections found in things are from one principle. Thus he says, **whether thrones or dominions** . . . , and so on. As if to say: They do not depend on an array of principles, but on the one unique Word of God.

41   Why does Paul say in his letter to the Ephesians (1:22) "He has made him the head over all the Church"? For he does not seem to be saying the same thing there as here. I reply that here Paul is giving a descending list of such beings, because he is showing the procession of creatures from God; but in Ephesians he gives an ascending list, because he is showing that the Son of God, as man, is above all creatures. In Ephesians, the principalities are placed under the authorities (or powers), and the virtues are between the dominions and authorities; but here in our text, the principalities are placed above the authorities, and between the dominions and the authorities. This is the way the teaching of Gregory differs from that of Dionysius. For Dionysius arranges the spiritual beings as they are in Ephesians, because he puts the dominions, the virtues, and the authorities in the second hierarchy. But Gregory arranges them as Paul does here, because he puts the dominions, principalities, and authorities in the second hierarchy; and the virtues, archangels, and the angels in the third hierarchy.

We should note, as Gregory and Dionysius say, that the spiritual gifts from which these different orders receive their names are common to all of them; yet some orders receive their name from certain of these gifts, and others receive their name from different gifts. The reason for this can be seen from the teachings of the Platonists: Whatever belongs to something belongs to it in one of three ways: essentially, or by participation, or causally. A thing belongs essentially to another if it belongs to it according to a certain proportion to its nature; this is the way to be rational belongs to man. A thing belongs by participation to another if it surpasses the nature of the thing that has it, although the thing participates to a certain extent in it, although imperfectly; thus man is intellectual by participation, while to be intellectual, which is superior to being rational, is in the angels essentially. One thing belongs to another causally if it accrues to it, as artifacts belong to a person; for they do not exist in him as in matter, but exist in his artistic power. Now a thing is named only from what belongs to it essentially; thus we do not define man as an intellectual or artistic being, but as a rational being.

In regard to the gifts present in the angels, those that belong to the higher angels essentially belong to the lower ones by participation; and those that belong to the lower ones essentially are present in the higher angels causally. Consequently, the higher angels receive their names from the higher gifts. But the highest thing in a spiritual creature is that it attain to God and somehow participate in him; and therefore the higher angels receive their name because they attain God: seraphim, as being fervent or on fire with God; the cherubim, as knowing God; and the thrones, as having God seated in them.

42 For one thing can participate in another in three ways: First, it can receive what is proper to the nature of what it is participating in; second, it can receive a thing insofar as it knows it; and third, it can somehow serve the power of a thing. For example, a doctor participates in the art of medicine either because he possesses in himself the art of medicine, or because he has received a knowledge of the art, or because he serves or devotes himself to the medical art. The first way of participating is greater than the second, and the second way is greater than the third.

In Sacred Scripture, what is divine is signified by fire: "The Lord your God is a devouring fire" (DEUT 4:24). And so the highest order of angels is called the seraphim, as though on fire with God and having a divine property. The second order is the cherubim, who attain God by knowledge. And the third are the thrones, that serve or are devoted to his power. The other orders are not given their names because they attain God, but because of some activity of God. Some angels direct or command, and these are the dominions. Others accomplish and carry out [what is commanded], the principal angels who do this are the principalities: "Princes went before, joined with singers" (Ps 68:27). Among the others who carry out commands, some act over spiritual creatures, such as the authorities (powers), who restrain the evil spirits. If some act over natural things, they are called virtues, and these perform miracles. If they act over human beings, they are called archangels if they are concerned with great matters and angels if concerned with lesser things.

And so Paul concludes, **all things were created through him** *[per ipsum]*, as by an efficient cause, **and in him** [in Thomas's text], as in an exemplary cause: "All things were made through him, and without him was not anything made that was made" (JN 1:3).

43   Since someone might ask: Are all things eternal? The Apostle says in answer: No! **He is before all**, that is, before all times and other things: "The Lord possessed me in the beginning of his ways, before he made anything from the beginning" (PROV 8:22). Or, **he is before all** in dignity: "Who among the heavenly beings is like the Lord?" (Ps 89:6).

44   As relating to the conservation of things he says, **and in him all things hold together**, that is, they are conserved. For God is to things as the sun is to the moon, which loses its light when the sun leaves. And so, if God took his power away from us, all things would immediately cease to exist: "Upholding the universe by his word of power" (HEB 1:3).

Chapter 1 ▪ Lectura 5

COLOSSIANS 1:18–23a

▪

¹⁸**HE is the head of the body, the church; he is the beginning, the first-born from the dead, that in everything he might be preeminent. ¹⁹For in him all the fulness of God was pleased to dwell, ²⁰and through him to reconcile to himself all things, whether on earth or in heaven, making peace by the blood of his cross. ²¹And you, who once were estranged and hostile in mind, doing evil deeds, ²²he has now reconciled in his body of flesh by his death, in order to present you holy and blameless and irreproachable before him, ²³provided that you continue in the faith, stable and steadfast, not shifting from the hope of the gospel which you heard, which has been preached to every creature under heaven.**

▪

45 After the Apostle commended Christ in his relationship to God and to all creatures, he here commends him in his relationship to the Church: first, in a general way; second, in particular, in reference to the Colossians (v. 21); and third, in reference to himself (v. 23b). In regard to the first he does two things: First, he mentions Christ's relationship to the entire Church; and second, he explains this relationship (v. 18b).

46 He says therefore that Christ, the first-born among creatures, is the one in whom we have our redemption. But because he has been made the head of the Church, two things have to be explained: first, in what way the Church is a body; and second, how Christ is its head.

The Church is called a body because of its likeness to a single human being. This likeness is twofold: first, in that it has distinct members: "And his gifts were that some should be apostles, some prophets, some evangelists, some pastors and teachers" (EPH 4:11); second, because the members of the Church serve each other in ways that are different: "The members may have the same care for one another" (1 COR 12:25); "Bear one another's burdens, and so fulfil the law of Christ" (GAL 6:2). Again, just as a body is one because its soul is one, so the Church is one because the Spirit is one: "There is one body and one Spirit" (EPH 4:4); "Because there is one bread, we who are many are one body, for we all partake of the one bread" (1 COR 10:17). Next we have to consider the relationship of the members to the head of the Church, that is, to Christ. For Christ is the head of the Church. "But you, O Lord, are the lifter of my head" (PS 3:3).

47 He explains what it means to be a head, saying, **he is the beginning, the first-born from the dead**. The head has three privileges over the other members of the body. First, it is superior in dignity, because it is a source and a ruler. Second, it has the fulness of the senses, which are all in the head. Third, it is the source of an inflow of sense and movement to the members of the body. So first, Paul shows how Christ is head because of his dignity; second, because of the fulness of his grace (V. 19); and third, because of an inflow from him (V. 20).

48 The Church exists in two states: the state of grace in the present time, and the state of glory in the future. But it is the same Church, and Christ is its head in both states, because he is the first in grace and the first in glory.

With respect to the first he says, **he is the beginning, the first-born from the dead**, because he is not only first in grace insofar as he is a man, but all men are justified by faith in Christ: "By one man's obedience many will be made righteous" (ROM 5:19). So he says, **he is the beginning** *[principium]*, that is, the beginning or source of justification and grace in the entire Church; because even in the Old Testament some were justified by faith in Christ: "I am the beginning who am speaking to you" (JN 8:25); "With you is the beginning" (PS 110:3) [Vulgate].

Christ is also the beginning of the state of glory; and so he says, **the first-born from the dead**. The reason for this is that the resurrection from the dead is a kind of second birth, because it restores us to eternal life: "In the rebirth, when the Son of Man sits on his glorious throne" (MT 19:28); but Christ is the first of all; and thus he is the first-born from the dead, that is, the first-born of those who are born by the resurrection.

49 But what about Lazarus (JN 11)? I answer that he and some others did not rise to the above-mentioned immortal life, but to a mortal life; but "Christ, having risen from the dead, will never die again" (ROM 6:9); "Jesus Christ, the first-born of the dead, and the ruler of kings on earth" (REV 1:5); "Christ has risen from the dead, the first fruits of those who have fallen asleep" (1 COR 15:20). And this is so **that in everything he might be preeminent**: preeminent in the gifts of grace, because he is the beginning; and preeminent in the gifts of glory, because he is the first-born: "In every nation I have had first place" (SIR 24:10) [Vulgate].

50 Then (V. 19) he shows the dignity of the head with respect to the fulness of all graces. For some saints had particular graces, but Christ had all graces; and so he says that **in him all the fulness was pleased to dwell** [it seems that Thomas's version lacked the words "of God"].

Each word has its own force. **Pleased** indicates that the gifts Christ had as man were not the result of fate or merits, as Photinus says, but were due to the good pleasure of the divine will taking this man into a unity of person: "This is my beloved Son, with whom I am well pleased" (MT 3:17). He says, **all**, because some have one gift and others different ones; but [with Christ] "the Father had given all things into his hands" (JN 13:3). He says, **fulness**, because one can have a gift without having the fulness of it or of its power, because perhaps one lacks something unwillingly. But John says that Christ was "full of grace and truth" (JN 1:14): "My abode is in the fulness of the saints" (SIR 24:16). He says **to dwell**, because some received the use of a grace for only a time; thus the spirit of prophecy was not always possessed by the prophets, but it is continuously present in Christ, because he always has control over this fulness to use it as he wishes: "He on whom you see the Spirit descend and remain, this is he who baptizes with the Holy Spirit" as we read in John (1:33).

51   Then when he says, **and through him to reconcile to himself all things,** he shows that Christ is the head of the Church because of an inflow from him. And this is the third characteristic of a head. First, he shows the inflow of grace; and second, he explains it.

52   He says therefore: I say that it pleased God not only that this fulness exist in Christ, but that it also flow from Christ to us; and so he says, **and through him to reconcile to himself all things**: "God was in Christ reconciling the world to himself" (2 COR 5:19).

53   He mentions the nature of this reconciliation and how all things are reconciled. Now there are two things to be considered in a reconciliation. First, the matters in which the reconciled persons agree. For people at odds have conflicting wills, but when they have been reconciled they agree in some things; and so wills that were before in conflict are made to harmonize in Christ. For example, the wills of men, of God, and of the angels. The will of men, because Christ is a man; and the will of God, because Christ is God. There was also conflict between the Jews, who wanted the law, and the Gentiles, who did not want the law. But Christ created harmony between the two, because he was from the Jews, and he freed us from the legal observances.

This harmony was accomplished **by the blood of his cross**. The cause of discord between God and men was sin; the discord between the Jews and the Gentiles was caused by the law. Now Christ destroyed sin by his cross and fulfiled the law; and thus he took away the causes of discord: "You have come to Mount Zion and to the city of the living God, the heavenly Jerusalem" (HEB 12:22). Thus we are reconciled and all things are set at peace, whether on earth, that is, Jews and Gentiles, or in heaven, that is, the angels and God. And so when Christ was born the angels sang: "Glory to God in the highest, and on earth peace among men" (LK 2:14). Again, Christ said at his resurrection: "Peace be with you" (JN 20:19); "For he is our peace, who has made us both one" (EPH 2:14).

54 Then (V. 21) Christ is commended because of the gifts he gave them. First, Paul recalls their past condition; second, Christ's gift (V. 22); and third, what they have to do now (V. 23).

55 Their past condition had three evils: In their intellect, they were ignorant; in their affections, they were enemies of justice; and in their actions, they committed many sins. In regard to the first he says, **estranged**; in regard to the second, **hostile in mind**, according to the reading of one version. This shows that there was a defect in that wisdom that the Jews proclaimed about the one God: "Men loved darkness rather than light" (JN 3:19). But were the Jewish people bound to the law of Moses? Yes they were, so far as it concerned the worship of the one God. Or, we could say the Jews were **estranged in mind**, that is, by choice, maliciously contradicting God: "They turned aside from following him" (JOB 34:27). As to the third evil of their past condition he says, **doing evil deeds**: "Their deeds were evil," as we read in John (3:19).

56 Then when he says, **he has now reconciled**, he mentions the benefits coming from Christ. The first of these is reconciliation in his body; and so he says, **he has now reconciled in his body of flesh**. He says, **his body of flesh**, not because his body and his flesh are not the same, but to show that Christ took a real body: "And the Word became flesh and dwelt among us" (JN 1:14). A **body of flesh**, that is, a mortal body: "God, sending his own Son in the likeness of sinful flesh and of sin, has condemned sin in the flesh" (ROM 8:3). The second benefit coming from Christ is holiness; thus he says, **in order to present you holy**: "So Jesus also suffered outside the gate in order to sanctify the people through his own blood" (HEB 13:12). The third benefit is their cleansing from sin; and as to this he says, **and blameless**: "The blood of Christ, who through the eternal Spirit offered himself without blemish to God, purifies your conscience from dead works" (HEB 9:14). Looking to the future he says, **irreproachable**: "Be zealous to be found by him without spot or blemish and at peace" (2 PET 3:14). And he adds, **before him**: "Man sees things that appear, but the Lord beholds the heart" (1 KG 16:7).

57 What God requires of us is that we be firm in faith and hope. And so, Paul continues, **provided that you continue in the faith, stable**. For faith is a foundation; if it is firm the entire structure of the Church is firm. And **steadfast** in hope, not weakening themselves from within; **not shifting** by allowing others to shake that hope. This hope, I say, is **the hope of the gospel**, that is, the hope that the Gospel gives for the good things of the kingdom of heaven: "Repent, for the kingdom of heaven is at hand" (MT 4:17).

And there is no excuse, because the Gospel **has been preached**; and he uses the past tense here instead of the future tense because this future event is so certain. The Gospel **has been preached**, by the apostles that is, **to every creature under heaven**, that is, to every new creature, that is, to the faithful, for whom it had been prepared.

Chapter 1 ▪ Lectura 6

COLOSSIANS 1:23b–29

‐‐‐‐‐‐‐‐‐‐‐‐‐‐‐‐‐‐‐‐ ■ ‐‐‐‐‐‐‐‐‐‐‐‐‐‐‐‐‐‐‐‐

²³ᵇ**AND of which I, Paul, became a minister.** ²⁴**Now I rejoice in my sufferings for your sake, and in my flesh I complete what is lacking in Christ's afflictions for the sake of his body, that is, the church,** ²⁵**of which I became a minister according to the divine office which was given to me for you, to make the word of God fully known,** ²⁶**the mystery hidden for ages and generations but now made manifest to his saints.** ²⁷**To them God chose to make known how great among the Gentiles are the riches of the glory of this mystery, which is Christ in you, the hope of glory.** ²⁸**Him we proclaim, warning every man and teaching every man in all wisdom, that we may present every man mature in Christ.** ²⁹**For this I toil, striving with all the energy which he mightily inspires within me.**

‐‐‐‐‐‐‐‐‐‐‐‐‐‐‐‐‐‐‐‐ ■ ‐‐‐‐‐‐‐‐‐‐‐‐‐‐‐‐‐‐‐‐

58 After Paul commended Christ in relation to God, to all creation, to the entire Church, and to the Colossians themselves, he now commends him in relation to himself, showing that he is Christ's minister. First, he mentions his ministry; second, he shows his faithfulness in it; and third, its greatness (V. 25).

59 He says, I say that the Gospel has been preached to all, the Gospel **of which I, Paul, became a minister**; to preach it, not on my own authority, but only as a minister: "This is how one should regard us, as servants of Christ and stewards of the mysteries of God" (1 COR 4:1).

60 He is a faithful minister. This is obvious, because he does not run away from the dangers involved in his preaching. First, he shows his attitude toward his sufferings; second, the fruit of his suffering (v. 24b). His attitude was one of joy, because **now I rejoice in my sufferings for your sake**, that is, for your benefit: "If we are afflicted it is for your comfort and salvation; and if we are comforted, it is for your comfort, which you experience when you patiently endure the same sufferings that we suffer" (2 COR 1:6). He also rejoices because of the joy of eternal life that he expects from them, and that is the fruit of his ministry: "Count it all joy, my brethren, when you meet various trials, for you know that the testimony of your faith produces steadfastness" (JAS 1:2): "Even if I am to be poured as a libation upon the sacrificial offering of your faith, I am glad and rejoice with you all" (PHIL 2:17).

61 And along with the above there is the fruit that **in my flesh I complete what is lacking in Christ's afflictions**. At first glance these words can be misunderstood to mean that the passion of Christ was not sufficient for our redemption, and that the sufferings of the saints were added to complete it. But this is heretical, because the blood of Christ is sufficient to redeem many worlds: "He is the expiation for our sins, and not for ours only but also for the sins of the whole world" (1 JN 2:2).

Rather, we should understand that Christ and the Church are one mystical person, whose head is Christ, and whose body is all the just, for every just person is a member of this head: "individually members" (1 COR 12:27). Now God in his predestination has arranged how much merit will exist throughout the entire Church, both in the head and in the members, just as he has predestined the number of the elect. And among these merits, the sufferings of the holy martyrs occupy a prominent place. For while the merits of Christ, the head, are infinite, each saint displays some merits in a limited degree.

This is why he says, **I complete what is lacking in Christ's afflictions**, that is, what is lacking in the afflictions of the whole Church, of which Christ is the head. I complete, that is, I add my own amount; and I do this in my flesh, that is, it is I myself who am suffering. Or, we could say that Paul was completing the sufferings that were lacking in his own flesh. For what was lacking was that, just as Christ had suffered in his own body, so he should also suffer in Paul, his member, and in similar ways in others.

And Paul does this **for the sake of his body**, which is the Church that was to be redeemed by Christ: "That he might present the Church to himself in splendor, without spot or wrinkle" (EPH 5:27). In the same way all the saints suffer for the Church, which receives strength from their example. The Gloss says that "afflictions are still lacking, because the treasure house of the Church's merits is not full, and it will not be full until the end of the world."

62   Then when he says, **of which I became a minister**, he shows the greatness of his ministry in three ways: first, from its origin; in the second place, from the end to which it is directed (V. 25b); and third, from its purpose (V. 28).

63   But someone could say: "Is his a great ministry?" He answers: Yes, because I became a minister because it was given to me **according to the divine office**. This can be explained in two ways. First in an active sense, and then the meaning is that I became a minister so that I could dispense divine things to you, faithfully passing them on; and this power has been given to me. Second, it can be explained in a passive sense, and then the meaning is that Paul became a minister insofar as he was appointed by

God. "And his gifts were that some should be apostles, some prophets, some evangelists, some pastors and teachers" (EPH 4:11); "Set apart for me Barnabas and Paul for the work to which I have called them" (ACTS 13:2).

64 What is the end of his ministry? Certainly, not money, or his own glory. Rather, he has received it for a great purpose, that is, **to make the word of God fully known**. First, he shows the greatness of that for which he has received this ministry; second, he shows what this is, namely, that it is Christ. He shows its greatness because it has been widely proclaimed, both in an obscure form and openly.

65 The ministry he received was to convert the Gentiles; thus, **to make fully known the word**, that is, the eternal dispensation of God. In other words, by my preaching I am to show that the word of God has been fulfiled, that is, God's dispensation and plan and promise concerning the incarnation of the Word of God. Or, I am to show by my preaching the eternal dispensation of God in which he arranged that the Gentiles were to be converted by Christ to a faith in the true God. And this had to be accomplished: "Does he say and not do? Does he speak and not do what he said?" (NUM 23:19); "My word that goes forth from my mouth shall not return to me empty, but it shall accomplish that which I purpose, and prosper in the thing for which I sent it," as we read in Isaiah (55:11).

66 But God arranged that this be accomplished by Paul's ministry, and so Paul says, **to make fully known this mystery** (it is called a mystery insofar as it is hidden), because this mystery, which has been hidden, is this word: "I have a secret, I have a secret" (IS 24:16) [Vulgate]. This mystery was **hidden for ages**, that is, from the beginning of the ages, and it was hidden from all the **generations** of men, who were unable to know this: "the plan of the mystery hidden for ages in God" (EPH 3:9).

For even though the early philosophers seem to have said something about Christ's divinity, either as being his own or appropriated (as Augustine found in the works of Plato, such as that "in the beginning was the Word," and things like that), yet none could know that the Word was made flesh. But you ask, was this not known by the prophets? I reply that it was, insofar as it pertained to the Gospel; but it was not known as explicitly as the apostles knew it.

67 Next, he deals with the revelation of this mystery. First, he shows to whom it was revealed; second, why it was revealed to them (v. 27).

68 He says that this mystery is **now made manifest**, that is, in this time of grace: "Behold now is the acceptable time, now is the day of salvation" (2 COR 6:2). This is the knowledge of the saints: "She gave him knowledge of holy things" (WIS 10:10); "He showed his friend that it belongs to him, and that he can approach it" (JOB 36:33) [Vulgate].

69 It was revealed to his saints not because of their own merits, but because of God's good pleasure; thus Paul says, to **them God chose to make known the riches of the glory of this mystery**: "All that I have heard from my Father I have made known to you. You did not choose me, but I chose you" (JN 15:15); "Yea, Father, for such was thy gracious will" (MT 11:26). To **make known the riches of the glory of this mystery**, because by the fact that such things had been hidden, God now appears superabundantly glorious. For God was formerly known in Judea, but through this mystery of the conversion of the Gentiles the glory of God is made known to the entire world: As we read in John (17:4), "I glorified you on earth." And this is to be done **among the Gentiles**, that is, it is to be accomplished among them: "Let us rejoice in our hope of sharing the glory of God" (ROM 5:2); "O the depth of the riches and wisdom and knowledge of God!" (ROM 11:33).

This mystery, **which is Christ**, that is, which we obtain through Christ, is the hope of glory, which had formerly been promised only to the Jews: "The believers from among the circumcised were amazed because the gift of the Holy Spirit had been poured out even on the Gentiles" (ACTS 10:45); "Justified by faith, let us have peace toward God; and let us glory in the hope of the glory of the sons of God" (ROM 5:1–2); "The root of Jesse, who stands as an ensign of the people, will be called on by the Gentiles" (IS 11:10). So far Paul has indicated the origin and end of his ministry.

70 Now he mentions its function. In regard to this he does three things. First, he indicates its function; second, its fruit (V. 28b); and in the third place, the help he was given (V. 29).

71 Its function is to announce Christ; and he shows this function and the method he used: "Announce his ways among the Gentiles" (PS 9:11); "That which we have seen and heard we proclaim also to you" (1 JN 1:1).

He states his method when he says, **warning every man**; this is a complete proclamation, because it is to every person, and not just the Jewish people: "Teach all nations" (MT 28:19). His method is to teach the truth and to refute what is false, and so he says, **warning every man**, or unbeliever, in this life: "The weapons of our warfare are not worldly but have divine power to destroy strongholds. We destroy arguments and every proud obstacle to the knowledge of God" (2 COR 10:4); and it also consists in **teaching every man in all wisdom**, which is the knowledge of God: "To know you is complete righteousness, and to know your power is the root of immortality" (WIS 15:3); "Among the mature we do impart wisdom" (1 COR 2:6).

72   The fruit of this in this life is that men are brought to perfection; and so he says, **that we may present every man**, that is, of any condition, **mature**, not in the law, but **in Christ**. "You, therefore, must be perfect, as your heavenly Father is perfect" (MT 5:48).

But is everyone bound to perfection? No, but it should be the goal of the preacher. Now the perfection of charity is of two kinds. One is from a necessity of precept, that is, that one not allow into his heart anything opposed to God: "You shall love the Lord your God with all your heart, and with all your soul, and with all your mind" (MT 22:37). The other perfection of charity is from a necessity of counsel, which is that one give up even those things that are lawful; and this kind of perfection goes beyond what is required. But for this Paul had God's help.

73   And so he says, **For this I toil, striving** against unbelievers and sinners: "Take your share of suffering as a good soldier of Christ Jesus" (2 TIM 2:3); "I have fought the good fight, I have finished the race, I have kept the faith" (2 TIM 4:7). And Paul does this **with all the energy**, "the grace of God is with me" (1 COR 15:10), **which he inspires within me**, because God does this in me **mightily**, that is, by giving me the might or power: "Stay in the city until you are clothed with power from on high," as we read in Luke (24:49).

Chapter 2 ▪ Lectura 1

COLOSSIANS 2:1–4

▪

¹**FOR I want you to know how greatly I strive for you, and for those at Laodicea, and for all who have not seen my face, ²that their hearts may be encouraged as they are knit together in love, to have all the riches of assured understanding and the knowledge of God's mystery, of Christ, ³in whom are hid all the treasures of wisdom and knowledge. ⁴I say this in order that no one may delude you with beguiling speech.**

▪

74 Above, Paul commended the condition of those who believe, that is, their state of grace, and its Author, Christ; here he protects them from what is opposed to this state. First, from teachings that destroy it; and second, from evil habits (CH. 3). In regard to the first he does two things. First, he shows his concern over their state, and second, he warns them against evil teachings (V. 4). The first part is again divided. First, he mentions his concern; second, the persons about whom he is concerned (V. 1b); and third, the matter that concerns him (V. 2).

75 Paul says, **I want you to know what concern I have** [Vulgate], that is, how great it is; and this is a mark of a good prelate: "to govern others with concern" (ROM 12:8); "And in that region there were shepherds out in the field, keeping watch over their flock by night" (LK 2:8).

76 His concern is not only for those whom he converted and who were with him, but also for others. And so he says, **for you**, whom I have not seen in person, but in my mind's eye. And his concern is also **for all who have not seen my face**. In fact, Paul cared about the whole world: "For upon his long robe the whole world was depicted" (WIS 18:24); "And, apart from other things, there is the daily pressure upon me of my anxiety for all of the churches" (2 COR 11:28).

But about whom was Paul most concerned? I answer that in a certain sense he was most concerned about those whom he could not see, because he did not know what was happening to them. But he was not concerned more about them in an absolute sense.

77 Then when he says, **that their hearts might be consoled, having been instructed in love, and in all the riches of a full understanding, so as to know the mystery of God, the Father, and of Jesus Christ** [Vulgate], he shows what he is concerned about, that is, their consolation. First, he mentions this; and second, he states how it can be brought about, **instructed in love**.

78 Paul says, **that their hearts might be consoled**, that is, that by means of me they might have spiritual consolation. Such consolation is produced by what is good, for when one is sad over something, it is a source of joy to be consoled by something equally good. Now there are two things that console us—meditation on wisdom: "She [that is, wisdom] would give me encouragement in cares and grief" (WIS 8:9); and prayer: "Is any one of you sad? Let him pray" (JAS 5:13).

79 Then when he says, **having been instructed in love**, he mentions their instruction in wisdom. There are two versions of this passage. First, the one we have here. Second, the one found in the Gloss: "that the hearts of those instructed in love might be consoled

. . ." so that they might know "the mystery of God, the Father, and of Jesus Christ." But the meaning is the same. When one is instructed in wisdom, he is consoled against temporal evils. But here a person should be instructed about the way; and so Paul says, in love, which is the way to God: "I will show you a still more excellent way. If I should speak in the tongues of men and of angels, but have not love, I am a noisy gong or a clanging cymbal" (1 COR 13:1).

Having been instructed in love, that is, in the love with which God loves us, and in the love with which we love him; for we are consoled by each of these loves. We are consoled because God loves us: "It is no longer I who live, but Christ who lives in me . . . who loved me and gave himself for me" (GAL 2:20); "Rich in mercy, out of the great love with which he loved us, even when we were dead through our trespasses, he made us alive together with Christ" (EPH 2:4). And we are also consoled because we love God, for it is consoling to a friend of God to endure evils for his sake: "If any evil happen to me because of him, I will bear it" (SIR 22:311) [Vulgate].

80   And Paul continues, **and in all the riches**, that is, to the extent of their capacity. Our intellect is in potency to know things, while the intellect of the angel was filled at its creation with a knowledge of understandable things. And so our human intellect must acquire its knowledge; and it does this either by study (and this is insufficient, because a thing can never be known so well so that it fulfils the capacity of our intellect); or it acquires its knowledge by a divine revelation and as a gift from God (and this is sufficient). "She [wisdom] will feed him with the bread of understanding, and give him the water of wisdom to drink" (SIR 15:3). And so he says, **of a full understanding**, that is, of an understanding in abundance: "What is richer than wisdom?" (WIS 8:5); "The riches of salvation are wisdom and knowledge" (IS 33:6).

In short, they are to be instructed with such an abundance of divine wisdom that it fulfils the capacity of their intellect. We will have this abundance of divine wisdom by knowing God; and so Paul says, **so as to know the mystery of God the Father and of Jesus Christ**, that is, to know the truth of this mystery that had been hidden, which is that God is the Father of Jesus Christ. Or, we could say, **to know the mystery of God the Father**, which mystery is Christ. And so Matthew says about the apostles: "You have hidden these things from the wise and understanding and revealed them to babes" (MT 11:25). Or, we will have this abundance of the divine wisdom by our knowledge of the eternal generation and of the incarnation of Christ: "To fix one's thought on her [wisdom] is perfect understanding" (WIS 6:15). As Augustine says, "Happy are those who know you, and unhappy those who do not." It is by knowing God that man has all fulness: "This is eternal life, that they know you the only true God, and Jesus Christ whom you have sent," as we read in John (17:4).

81   But is our intellect filled by knowing Christ? I say that it is because in him **are hid all the treasures of wisdom and knowledge**. God has a knowledge of all things, and this knowledge is called a treasure: "It is an unfailing treasure for men; those who get it obtain friendship with God" (WIS 7:14).

Now a treasure is a collection of riches; they are not called a treasure when scattered about, but only when collected in one place. "God has poured out his wisdom upon all his works" (SIR 1:10) [Vulgate]; from this point of view his wisdom does not have the nature of a treasure. But his wisdom is a treasure when the ideas behind all his works are considered collected together, that is, in the divine wisdom. And all such treasures are in Christ. Wisdom is the knowledge of divine things, and science *[scientia]* is the knowledge of created things. Now whatever can be known about God, which pertains to wisdom, God knows in himself, and exhaustively. And likewise, whatever can be known about created things, God knows in himself, and in an super-eminent way.

Now whatever is in the wisdom of God is in his single Word, because he knows all things by one simple act of his intellect, for in God knowledge is neither in potency nor in a habitual state. And thus in this Word **are all the treasures of wisdom and knowledge** *[sapientia et scientia]*.

82   He adds that these treasures are hid, because there are two reasons why something might be hidden from me: either because my intellect is weak, or because the thing is somehow covered. Thus, a person may not see a candle either because he is blind, or because the candle has been covered. And so, in the Word of God there are **all the treasures of wisdom and knowledge**, but they are hid from us because our eyes are not clear but bleary: "A little light is in you" (JN 12:35); and they are hid because they are covered with two veils: the veil of creatures, because at this time our intellect cannot come to this knowledge except through the likeness of creatures: "Ever since the creation of the world his invisible nature, namely, his eternal power and deity, has been clearly perceived in the things that have been made" (ROM 1:20); and the veil of the flesh: "The Word became flesh" (JN 1:14). And even if we do know something about God, yet we do not see all: "Truly, you are a God who hides yourself" (IS 45:15); "Open your treasure for him" (NUM 20:6).

Let us suppose that a person has a candle that is covered; he would not look then for another light, but wait for the light he has to become uncovered. And in the same way we do not have to look for wisdom anywhere but in Christ: "For I decided to know nothing among you except Jesus Christ and him crucified" (1 COR 2:2). And we read in 1 John (3:2): "When he appears," that is, is revealed, "we shall be like him," that is, knowing all things. In other words, if I had a book in which all knowledge was contained, I would seek to know only that book; similarly, it is not necessary for us to seek any further than Christ.

83 Then (V. 4) he teaches and warns them about destructive doctrines. For they were being misled by certain philosophers in matters against the faith, and by heretics who taught that the ceremonies of the law had to be observed. First, he teaches them in opposition to the philosophers; and second, in opposition to the Judaizers (V. 11).

In worldly knowledge there are two things: a knowledge of the spoken language, and a knowledge of things themselves. And so they could be deceived in two ways. Thus he first warns them against those philosophers who were deceiving them by their ability to speak well; and second, against those who were misleading them about the knowledge of things, when he says, "See to it that no one makes a prey of you by philosophy and empty deceit" (2:8). First, he mentions this deception; and second, the reason for it (V. 5).

84 Thus he says: I say that in Christ there is all knowledge. And I say this so that you will not be deceived in seeking for knowledge from anywhere else. And he says, **I say this in order that no one**, that is, neither Demosthenes or Cicero, **may delude you with beguiling speech**. "You will see no more the insolent people, the people of an obscure speech which you cannot comprehend, stammering in a tongue which you cannot understand" (Is 33:19).

85 But is it a sin to use beautiful language? I answer that it is not, because even saintly men, like Ambrose, Jerome, and Pope Leo, speak with more eloquence than the orators of this world. For if one can use fine language to persuade those who are evil, then it can be used much more to convince those who are good.

Chapter 2 ▪ Lectura 2

COLOSSIANS 2:5–10

▪

---

⁵**FOR though I am absent in body, yet I am with you in spirit, rejoicing to see your good order and the firmness of your faith in Christ. ⁶As therefore you received Christ Jesus the Lord, so live in him, ⁷rooted and built up in him and established in the faith, just as you were taught, abounding in thanksgiving. ⁸See to it that no one makes a prey of you by philosophy and empty deceit, according to human tradition, according to the elemental spirits of the universe, and not according to Christ. ⁹For in him the whole fulness of deity dwells bodily, ¹⁰and you have come to fulness of life in him, who is the head of all rule and authority.**

▪

---

86 Above, he warned them against falling away from the faith as a result of some deceptive language; here he gives the reason for this advice, which is based on the good things they have and should not destroy, but allow to grow. First, he calls to mind the goods that they have; and second, he shows how these should grow within them (v. 6). In regard to the first, he does two things. First, he shows how he happens to know about the good things they have; second, he mentions what these goods are (v. 5b).

87 Paul says, **For though I am absent in body, yet I am with you in spirit, rejoicing**. He is here saying, in effect, that although

I have not preached to you, nor do I see with my own eyes what you have accomplished, yet I am with you in spirit through my love, rejoicing in your blessings: "For though absent in body I am present in spirit" (1 COR 5:3); "A wise son makes a glad father" (PR 10:1). And this because it was revealed to him by the Holy Spirit; and so he says, **yet I am with you in spirit**. "Did I not go with you in spirit when the man turned from his chariot to meet you?" (2 KG 5:26).

88   **Rejoicing**, I say, because **I see your good order**, that is, your well-ordered way of life: "All things should be done decently and in order" (1 COR 14:40); "The stars remaining in their order and courses fought against Sisera" (JG 5:20). And rejoicing in **the firmness of your faith in Christ**: "God's firm foundation stands" (2 TIM 2:19). And this **in Christ**: "That Christ may dwell in your hearts through faith, rooted and founded in love" (EPH 3:17); "In whom the whole structure is joined together and grows into a holy temple in the Lord" (EPH 2:21). The goodness of this temple consists in its firm foundation, which is faith, and in a proper superstructure; and that is why he mentioned these two.

89   Then (v. 6) he urges them to protect these goods: first, by advancing in them; second, by their perseverance; and third, by giving thanks.

So he says, **As therefore you received Christ Jesus**, not in a distorted way, so **live in him**. "Hold fast to what is good," as we read in Romans (12:9). Sometimes the Church is compared to a spiritual building: "God's temple is holy, and that temple you are" (1 COR 3:17). At other times it is compared to a tree because it produces fruit. Now the foundation of a building is related to the building as the roots of a tree are related to the tree because the foundation and roots are the source of strength; and this source is Christ. "In that day the root of Jesse shall stand as an ensign to the peoples" (Is 11:10); "For no other foundation can any one lay than that which is laid, which is Jesus Christ" (1 COR 3:11).

So Paul uses the expression, **rooted**, like good branches, and **built up in him and established**, like good stones. And they will be like this if they persevere **in the faith**: "Your adversary, the devil, prowls around like a roaring lion, seeking some one to devour" (1 PET 5:8); and the text continues: "Resist him, firm in your faith." They are to live in Christ **just as you were taught**, that is, in the true faith: "If any one is preaching to you a gospel contrary to that which you received, let him be accursed" (GAL 1:9). **Abounding in thanksgiving**, giving many thanks: as we read in 1 Thessalonians (5:18), "Giving thanks in all circumstances"; "Having been saved by God out of grave dangers, we give him great thanks" (2 MACC 1:11).

90 Then (V. 8) he warns them not to be deceived by an empty wisdom. First, we see his warning; and second, the reason for it (V. 9). In regard to the first, he first teaches them to avoid whatever can deceive them; and second, the source of this deception (V. 8b).

91 A person can be deceived by worldly wisdom in two ways, that is, sometimes by the real principles of philosophy, and sometimes by fallacious arguments. And Paul teaches them to beware of both: **See to it that no one makes a prey of you by philosophy**, that is, by philosophical teachings: "Your wisdom and your knowledge led you astray" (IS 47:10). For there are many who have turned from the faith after having been deceived by philosophy: "Man has become foolish in his knowledge" (JER 10:14). As regards to the second way to be deceived he says, **and empty deceit**, which is based on the way words are used: "Let no one deceive you with empty words," as is said in Ephesians (5:6).

92 But how are they being deceived? One who deceives another must have something that seems reasonable, and something that is not really so. So first Paul shows the basis of this seeming reasonableness. It is based on two things, the first being the authority of the philosophers. And about this he says, **according to human tradition**, that is, according to what is handed down by some, basing themselves on their own judgment: "The Lord knows the thoughts of man, that they are but a breath" (PS 94:11).

The second source of an apparent reasonableness are the contrivances of reason, that is, when a person wishes to measure or judge about the things of faith according to the principles of things, and not by divine wisdom. And many are deceived in this way. And so Paul says, they should not be deceived by those judging **according to the elements of the universe, and not according to Christ**: "They were unable from the good things that are seen to know him who exists" (WIS 13:1). Now the higher a cause is, the more superior is its effect. And so those who wish to investigate certain effects in terms of causes that are inferior are deceived. For example, if one were to consider the movement of water in terms of the power of water, he would not be able to know the cause of the tides of the sea; to do this he would have to consider water in terms of the power of the moon. Thus, those people are even more deceived who consider the proper effects of God in terms of the elements of the world. And this is the reason for the seeming plausibility of what they say.

93   But is it possible that the traditions and explanations of men are always to be rejected? I respond: No, but only when natural reason proceeds according to those traditions and explanations, and not according to Christ. As also below (2:19): "not holding fast to the Head from whom the whole body, nourished and knit together through its joints and ligaments, grows with a growth that is from God."

94   Or, we could say that **according to the elements of the universe** means, by measuring the truth of faith according to the truth of creatures. Or perhaps Paul said this referring to the idolaters who were worshiping idols and saying that Jupiter was the heavens. Or, Paul was referring to the Jewish people, and then the text is understood this way: **by philosophy**, by the reasoning of those who were trying to convince them to observe the ceremonies of the law, and these, **according to the elements of the universe** or world, that is, according to the bodily observances: "We were slaves to the elements of the world" (GAL 4:3). But our first explanation is better.

95   Then when he says, **For in him the whole fulness of deity dwells bodily**, he gives the reason for what he has just stated, saying that whatever is not according to Christ should be rejected. But is Christ so good that all things should be rejected for him? He answers that he is, and shows it in three ways: first, by considering his divinity; second, by his relationship to those who believe (V. 10a); and third, by his relationship to the angels (V. 10b).

96   So he says, whatever is contrary to Christ must be rejected, because he is God. Thus we must prefer him to everything else, **for in him the whole fulness of deity dwells bodily**. Now God is in all things. He is in some things because they participate in a likeness to his goodness, as a stone and things like that. Such things are not God, but they have in themselves something of God; not his substance, but a likeness of his goodness. Consequently, the fulness of divinity does not dwell in them, because he is not there according to his substance. Again, he is in holy minds by an activity, minds that attain God by love and knowledge; and thus God is in them by grace, not bodily, but according to the effect of grace. And he is not there in his fulness, but only by some limited effects. But God is present in Christ bodily; and this is explained in three ways.

97 A body is distinguished from its shadow: "These are only a shadow of what is to come; but the substance belongs to Christ" (HEB 2:17). And so God can indwell in two ways, either as a shadow or bodily, that is, really. The first way is the way he dwelt in the Old Law, but in Christ he dwells bodily, that is, really and truly.

This passage is explained in a second way by saying that God dwells in the other saints only with respect to their souls, and not in their bodies: "For I know that nothing good dwells within me, that is, in my flesh" (ROM 7:18). But the divinity dwells in Christ bodily, because the indwelling of God in the saints is by an activity, that is, by love and knowledge, which are actions of a rational mind alone, but God dwells in Christ by assuming a man into the unity of his person. And thus whatever relates to this man is indwelt by God; and thus his flesh and mind are indwelt because both are united to the Word: "And the Word became flesh" (JN 1:14).

The third explanation of this passage is as follows: God is in things in three ways. One way is common, that is, by his power, presence, and essence. He is present in another way in the saints, that is, by grace. The third way is found only in Christ, and he is present here by union. Now a body has three dimensions, and the fulness of the divinity superabounds in Christ in these ways. And so the deity is said to be in him bodily. The fulness of the divinity is in Christ, as it were, by length, because it extends to all things; it is in him by breadth, that is, in its charity; and it is in him in its depth, that is, in its incomprehensibility.

98 Nestorius was mistaken on this point: He said that this union was brought about entirely by an indwelling, the Word dwelling in the flesh. But the Apostle does not agree with this, for he says in Philippians (2:7): "He emptied himself, taking the form of a servant." Now when one dwells in a man he does not empty himself; one empties oneself by becoming man. And so Paul continues, "being born in the likeness of man." And so Christ is indwelt, but not in the sense that the one indwelling and the one dwelt in are distinct, but in the sense that Christ is both man and God, in whom dwells the fulness of the deity.

99 Then when he says, **and you have come to fulness in him**, he shows the same thing by relating Christ to others. He is saying, in effect: You have received all things: "From his fulness have we all received" (JN 1:16).

We should note that the Platonists teach that all divine gifts come to men by the mediation of the separated substances; and this is true even according to Dionysius. But this is something special, that we receive divine gifts immediately from him who is the fulness of the angels: "The only Son who is in the bosom of the Father, he has made him known" (JN 1:18); "It was declared at first by the Lord, and it was attested to us by those who heard him" (HEB 2:3).

100 And so Paul continues, **who is the head of all rule and authority** [or, "principality and power," two orders of angels], insofar as he is their King and Lord, not by a likeness of nature, because that is the way he is the head of man. And Paul mentions those orders [of angels] that seem to have a certain preeminence.

Chapter 2 ■ Lectura 3

COLOSSIANS 2:11–15

---

¹¹**IN him also you were circumcised with a circumcision made without hands, by putting off the body of flesh in the circumcision of Christ; ¹²and you were buried with him in baptism, in which you were also raised with him through faith in the working of God, who raised him from the dead. ¹³And you, who were dead in trespasses and the uncircumcision of your flesh, God made alive together with him, having forgiven us all our trespasses, ¹⁴having canceled the bond which stood against us with its legal demands; this he set aside, nailing it to the cross. ¹⁵He disarmed the principalities and powers and made a public example of them, triumphing over them in him.**

---

101   Above, Paul warned the faithful against the deceptions of the worldly philosophers; here he instructs and warns them against those heretics who wanted to drag them into the observances of the law. First, he instructs them to avoid such persons; second, he rejects the false enticements they used (V. 18). In regard to the first, he does two things: First, he shows that the observances of the law were completed in Christ; and second, he rejects these observances, showing that they are not bound to follow them (V. 16).

102 Among the observances of the law, the first was circumcision. By this, the Jews professed their observance of the Old Law, just as we profess our observance of the New Law by baptism: "I testify again to every man who receives circumcision that he is bound to keep the whole law" (GAL 5:3). So Paul says that the faithful have been circumcised with a certain spiritual circumcision, from which it follows that the other has ceased. First, he shows what kind of circumcision they have received; and second, how it was received. Finally, he tells why they were circumcised in this way (V. 13).

103 In regard to the first, we should note that there are two kinds of circumcision, bodily and spiritual. We have been circumcised by Christ with a spiritual circumcision, and not by the bodily kind. So first Paul eliminates such a bodily circumcision, and then explains about this spiritual circumcision.

Paul continues: In him, that is, in Christ, **you were circumcised with a circumcision made without hands**: "For he is not a real Jew who is one outwardly, nor is true circumcision something external and physical. He is a Jew who is one inwardly, and real circumcision is a matter of the heart, spiritual and not literal" (ROM 2:28).

104 **By putting off the body of flesh**. This can be understood in two ways. In the first way Paul says that **you were circumcised with a circumcision made without hands, by putting off the body of flesh**, that is, by putting off the corruption of the flesh, as mentioned in 1 Corinthians (15:50): "Flesh and blood cannot inherit the kingdom of God, nor does the perishable inherit the imperishable." He is saying in effect: You have been circumcised because you no longer have the vices of the flesh: "You have put off the old nature with its practices" (COL 3:9). Another explanation would be: You have been circumcised **with a circumcision made not with hands**, which circumcision made with hands consists in a **putting off the body of flesh** that is cut from it.

And so in another version of this passage we find "skin of the flesh," instead of "body of flesh," that is, putting off a small part of the body that is flesh. (The meaning is not that the body is one thing and the flesh another.) Paul uses the word "flesh" to refer us back to the law, where it speaks of flesh: "You shall be circumcised in the flesh of your foreskins" (GEN 17:11). He uses this word also to show that it is a carnal observance.

105   But we are not circumcised in that [physical] way, but with **the circumcision of Christ**. For just as Christ accepted a likeness to sinful flesh, that is, flesh that could suffer, in order to free us from sin, so he also accepted the remedies contained in the law, so that he could free us from the observances of the law. Or, we could interpret **the circumcision of Christ** to mean the circumcision that Christ accomplishes in us, which is a spiritual circumcision, as Romans (2:29) says: "spiritual and not literal."

106   Second, he shows that we have received this circumcision in baptism, and so baptism is a spiritual circumcision. And first, he shows that in baptism we have a symbol of Christ's death; second, that in baptism we receive a likeness to his resurrection (V. 12b).

107   So Paul says: **and you were buried with him in baptism**, because in our baptism we find a likeness to Christ's death, and it is this: Just as Christ was put into the tomb, after having been put on the cross, so a person who is baptized is put under the water, and this is done three times, just as Christ was three days in the tomb. Again, **you were buried with him in baptism**, that is, your baptism was like the death of Christ, for as his death destroyed sin, so also does your baptism.

108   And just as Christ rose from the tomb, so we rise from our sins in the present, and from the corruption of the flesh in hope.

This is accomplished **through faith in the working of God**, because it was by the power of God that Christ was raised: "Raise me up, that I may requite them" (Ps 41:10). And by believing in this resurrection we come to share in it: "He who raised Christ Jesus from the dead will give life to your mortal bodies" (Rom 8:11). But Christ also raised himself, because the action of the Father and of the Son is the same: "I will awake the dawn" (Ps 108:2).

109   Then (v. 13), he shows the nature of this likeness. First, he states the likeness; and second, how we are freed from our sins (v. 14).

110   The text is not difficult. I said that you have been circumcised, because you have been buried, in baptism, with Christ. And he compared baptism to the burial and death of Christ. Yet one could say that it would be more to the point to say that Paul first shows that baptism is a circumcision. And second, he shows why it is a circumcision, that is, because sin is superfluous and the foreskin is superfluous. And so to remove sin and to remove the foreskin are the same. Now sin is removed in baptism. Therefore, baptism is the same as a circumcision. And so Paul says, **and you, who were dead in trespasses**, that is, because of your sins: "The death of sinners is the worst" (Ps 34:21), **and in the uncircumcision of your flesh**, that is, in your carnal concupiscence, which is related to original sin, as though they were chained with a debt of evil actions and of mortal sin.

111   **God made you alive**: "God, when we were dead through our trespasses, made us alive together with Christ" (Eph 2:5). He made you alive by removing every sin from you, forgiving and remitting all your faults. Thus, to be circumcised is the same as to be made alive, for the same baptism removes the death of sin and circumcises us by cutting off original sin.

112   But how has God forgiven us? I answer that a person incurs two things by sinning, that is, a debt of guilt, and slavery to the devil. And so he explains how sins are forgiven: first, our being freed from slavery to the devil, and second, he mentions the removing of the debt of guilt.

113   He says, **having canceled the bond that stood against us**; this bond or written decree can be understood in two ways. In one way it is the Old Law: "By abolishing in his flesh the law of commandments and ordinances, that he might create in himself one new man in place of the two" (EPH 2:15). This is its meaning when he is here speaking in reference to the Jews, as if to say: **and you . . . God made alive**. Again, a written bond is a warranty usually employed in contracts. And whoever violates God's bond is subject to a debt of punishment. This violation is retained in the person's memory, which it disturbs and stains; it is retained in God's memory, who is to judge such matters; and in the memory of the devils, who will torment them. Now the memory of this violation is called a bond. And it is Christ who has forgiven all by having canceled the bond, that is, the memory of the transgression, **which stood against us**. The bond, in both its meanings, was against us: the Law, because it gave mankind a knowledge of sin, but did not help [in overcoming sin], and the memory of our transgressions, for which we deserved to be punished.

The term **bond** is used because its violation is not forgiven in such a way as to bring it about that there was never any sin. Rather, such sin is not remembered by God as something to be punished; it is not remembered by the devils as something to accuse us of; and we do not remember our sins as reasons for sorrow: "Blessed is he whose transgression is forgiven, whose sin is covered" (PS 32:1).

114   Another interpretation of this passage would be that Paul is here speaking in general, to all, not just about the Jews. And then we can say that a command was given to the first man: "You may freely eat of every tree of the garden; but of the tree of knowledge of good and evil you shall not eat, for in the day that you eat of it you shall die" (GEN 2:16). But man violated this law, and the memory of this violation became a bond that stood against us. And Christ canceled this.

115   How did Christ cancel this bond? On the cross, for **this he set aside, nailing it to the cross**. It was the custom for a bond to be torn up once a person had fulfiled all his obligations. Now man was in sin and Christ paid for this by his suffering: "What I did not steal must I now restore?" (PS 69:4). And therefore, at the moment of Christ's death this bond was canceled and destroyed. And so he says, **this he set aside, nailing it to the cross**, by which he took away our sin by making satisfaction to God.

116   Then (V. 15) he shows how Christ freed us from the slavery of sin. For if a creditor holds a man captive on account of a debt that he owes, it is not enough merely to pay the debt; the person himself must also be freed. This is what Christ did. So Paul says, **he disarmed** [rather, "despoiled"] **the principalities and powers**. This despoiling can refer to those saints who had died before Christ's passion; in this sense, Christ freed them from the lower world by despoiling the devil: "As for you also, because of the blood of my covenant with you, I will set your captives free from the waterless pit" (ZECH 9:11); "Even the captives of the mighty shall be taken, and the prey of the tyrant be rescued" (IS 49:25). But if we understand this as referring to the living, then he despoiled them from the devils: "But when one stronger than he assails him and overcomes him, he takes away his armor in which he trusted, and divides his spoil" (LK 11:22); "Now shall the ruler of this world be cast out" (JN 12:31).

Thus he says, **he despoiled the principalities and powers**, that is, the devils themselves: "Against the principalities, against the powers, against the world rulers of this present darkness, against the spiritual hosts of wickedness in heavenly places" (EPH 6:12). **And made a public example of them**, that is, the saints, as one who had authority in heaven, over the dead and the living, in the kingdom of his glory or of his grace. Or we could say **he made a public example of them**, that is, he drove out the principalities from mankind, "Awake, and put on strength, O arm of the Lord" (IS 51:9), and with a public judgment, so it could be known that they were expelled. For at one time the world did serve idols, but not now. Or we could say there was a **public example**, that is, before the multitude of angels, because Christ descended into the lower world of the saints and ascended into heaven.

Triumphing over them in him, that is, in himself, in his own power. "By the power which enables him even to subject all things to himself" (PHIL 3:21).

117   Another version of this passage reads: "He put off his flesh, and exemplified the principalities and powers, triumphing confidently." "He put off his flesh," that is, his mortality. "Flesh and blood," that is, the mortality of bodily corruption, "cannot inherit the kingdom of God" (1 COR 15:50); "Christ being raised from the dead will never die again; death no longer has dominion over him" (ROM 6:9); "Even though we once regarded Christ from a human point of view, we regard him thus no longer" (2 COR 5:16). "He exemplified," he gave us an example of how the principalities and powers are to be overcome. The meaning of the rest stays the same.

Chapter 2 ▪ Lectura 4

COLOSSIANS 2:16–23

---

^{16}THEREFORE let no one pass judgment on you in questions of food and drink or with regard to a festival or a new moon or a sabbath. ^{17}These are only a shadow of what is to come; but the substance belongs to Christ. ^{18}Let no one disqualify you, insisting on self-abasement and worship of angels, taking his stand on visions, puffed up without reason by his sensuous mind, ^{19}and not holding fast to the Head, from whom the whole body, nourished and knit together through its joints and ligaments, grows with a growth that is from God. ^{20}If with Christ you died to the elemental spirits of the universe, why do you live as if you still belonged to the world? Why do you submit to regulations, ^{21}"Do not handle, Do not taste, Do not touch" ^{22}(referring to things which all perish as they are used), according to human precepts and doctrines? ^{23}These have indeed an appearance of wisdom in promoting rigor of devotion and self-abasement and severity to the body, but they are of no value, serving only to indulge the flesh.

---

118 Above, Paul showed that the law was fulfiled in Christ because of the circumcision he received, for this is an acknowledgment of the law. Here, he concludes that they are not obliged to observe the ceremonial commands of the law. There were four kinds of ceremonial matters: sacrifices, sacred things, sacraments, and observances. The sacrifices were those things that were immolated to God, such as sheep, oxen, and the like. The sacred things included utensils and religious festivals. There were three sacraments: circumcision, the paschal lamb, and the consecration of priests. The observances were those matters that were related to the unique customs in the life of the people of Israel, things such as food, clothing, and the like. Some of the above matters, such as the sacrifices, the utensils, and so on, pertained only to some of the people; other matters were connected to all the people. Paul does not mention those things that pertained just to some, but only those that affected all, just as baptism now affects us all.

119   He does mention the observances, because they abstained from certain foods, such as four-legged animals that do not have a divided hoof (LEV 11:26). In regard to drink, a vessel without a cover was unclean, as was anything in it. And so with respect to these matters he says, **let no one pass judgment on you in questions of food and drink**, that is, let no one condemn you for taking food and drink forbidden in the law: "Let not him who abstains pass judgment on him who eats; for God has welcomed him" (ROM 14:3).

120   He also mentions sacred matters related to the religious festivals and ceremonies. Under the Old Law there were continuous religious ceremonies, like the morning and evening sacrifices. There were other ceremonies held at certain definite times. Some of these were held several times during the year, as the sabbath every week, and the new moon every month. Others came only once a year, as the Passover, the Feast of Tabernacles, and Pentecost.

The reason for this is that all religious ceremonies are held for the honor of God. Now we give honor to God either because of something that is eternal, and thus we have continuous religious ceremonies; or we honor him because of certain temporal benefits that affect all people. There are two such benefits. First, the gift of creation; and thus we have the religious ceremony of the sabbath: "Remember the sabbath day, to keep it holy" (EX 20:8). The reason for keeping the sabbath is that God rested on the seventh day. The allegorical reason for the sabbath is that it signifies Christ's rest in the tomb, and the anagogical reason would be that it signifies the soul's rest in God. The other gift is that of procreation and preservation, which are also for a time. And since the Jewish people calculated the time by the moon, he says, a new moon. There are also other reasons for honoring God, as a special rescue or deliverance; and so other festivals were added to the above. And so he says, **or with regard to a festival or a new moon**, every month, or **sabbath[s]**, every seventh period. He says **sabbath[s]** because a sabbath is a rest, and they had several sabbaths: the seventh day; and seven weeks, that is Pentecost, which is the end of the seventh week following the Passover, which is the beginning of the year; and the seventh month; and the seventh year, when sins are forgiven; and after seven periods of seven years there was a Jubilee. With this in mind Paul says, **or sabbath[s]**, meaning: Let no one condemn you for not observing these feasts.

121   For **these are only a shadow of what is to come**, that is, of Christ. And when the truth comes, the shadow should cease, **but the substance belongs to Christ**. When someone sees a shadow, he expects the body or substantial reality to follow. Now the legal observances of the law were the shadow going before Christ, and they signified his coming; and so Paul says, **the substance**, that is, the truth of the thing, belongs to Christ, but the shadow belongs to the law.

122   Then (V. 18) he speaks against those who were trying to seduce and deceive them. First, he warns them not to be misled;

second, he argues against those already misled (v. 20). As to the first, he cautions them about being misled; second, he shows how they might be deceived, **insisting on self-abasement**; and third, the shortcomings of those who would mislead them (18b).

123   He says, **let no one [seduce] you** away from the truth that I have told you: "Let no one deceive you with empty words" (Eph 5:6).

124   For these pseudoapostles were seducing them by their "humility," bringing in observances taken from the law, for they pretended to be holy. But holiness consists of two things: a humble manner of life, and the worship of God. Now these people appeared to lead a humble life since they seemed to have no care for the things of the world; and so Paul says they were **insisting on self-abasement**. "There is one who is humble in an evil way, and within he is full of deceit" (Sir 19:23). Again, they claimed to be preaching out of reverence for God; and so Paul says, **and [religion] of angels**: for religion, according to Cicero, consists in ceremonies and worship for a divine nature: "Holding the form of religion but denying the power of it" (2 Tim 3:5).

125   The Gloss has this passage as reading, "in the religion of angels," for in this way these seducers wanted to seem like angels, that is, as messengers, of God: "Beware of false prophets, who come to you in sheep's clothing yet inwardly are ravenous wolves" (Mt 7:15). Or, "in the religion of angels," can be understood in a literal sense, because the Old Law was made known by angels, as we see from Galatians (3:19); "For if the message declared by angels was valid and every transgression or disobedience received a just retribution, how shall we escape if we neglect such a great salvation?" (Heb 2:2). These people maintained that the worship mandated in the law had to be kept, because it had been given through angels.

126   The shortcomings of such people were threefold; they were defective in their knowledge, in their justice, and in their faith. As to their knowledge, Paul says that such a person was **taking his stand on [things that were not seen]**, that is, things that were not understood. Such a one did not know why the law was given: "Desiring to be teachers of the law, without understanding either what they are saying or the things about which they make assertions" (1 TIM 1:7).

127   As to the justice of such persons he says they were **puffed up without reason**, in vain, although they pretended to be humble. And he mentions two things. First, that their religion was useless, because they went about without reason, in vain, that is, doing things that were of no value for eternal life: "Their labors are unprofitable" (WIS 3:11); "Though her labor be in vain, yet she has no fear restraining her" (JOB 39:16).

They also showed a false humility, and so he says that such a one was **puffed up by his sensuous mind**. There is a difference between one who is puffed up and one who is robust. A person who is robust is full with truth, while one who is puffed up is empty and just extended with wind. Therefore, those who are truly humble are full, but those who are only puffed up are empty. "He will burst those who are puffed up" (WIS 4:19) [Vulgate]. This is the meaning of 1 Corinthians (8:1): "Knowledge puffs up."

128   With regard to their faith he says that they were **not holding fast to the Head**, that is, Christ, by faith. Such people are deceived, because without Christ they are in the dark: "If any one does not agree with the sound words of our Lord Jesus Christ and the teaching which accords with godliness, he is puffed up with conceit, he knows nothing" (1 TIM 6:3).

129 Why is Christ the Head? Paul answers: Because the entire good of the body, which is the Church, depends on him. For there are two goods in a natural body: the union or joining together of its members and its growth. And the Church obtains these from Christ, for the entire body depends on him: "We, though many, are one body in Christ" (ROM 12:5). In a body the members are joined in two ways. One way is by contact, as the hand is joined to the wrist, and the wrist to the forearm, and so on. The other is by a connection, as being joined by nerves. And so Paul refers to **joints and ligaments**. So also in the Church, its members are joined by faith and understanding: "One Lord, one faith, one baptism" (EPH 4:5). But this is incomplete without the ligaments of charity and the sacraments. Thus Paul says, **nourished through ligaments**, because it is through charity that one person supplies another.

This body is developed by Christ, because it **grows with a growth that is from God**, that is, with a growth that God produces in us: "Blessed are the men whose strength is in you, . . . they go from strength to strength" (PS 84:5). Or, **from God**, that is, from Christ, who, as God, increases the body, the Church being enlarged: "For the equipment of the saints, for the work of the ministry, for building up the body of Christ" (EPH 4:12).

130 Then (V. 20) he rebukes those who have already been deceived. First, he bases the reason for his rebuke on the condition of those who have been deceived; and second, on the matters about which they were misled (22).

131 Their condition was one of freedom, because just as they were dead to sin, so also they were dead to the law. Thus they were not obliged to keep it. Paul says, therefore, **If with Christ you died**, being dead to the law, **to the [elements]**, that is, to the observances of the law (for the Jewish people served the true God, but under the elements; while the Gentiles served the elements themselves), why, since you know the truth, **do you live as if you still belonged to the world**, like the Jews live? **Why do you submit to regulations** about what is to be handled and eaten; regulations such as **do not handle**, because it is a sin; **do not taste** pork or eels (LEV 11:7,11)?

132   Then (V. 22) he describes these legal observances, saying that they are harmful, vain, and burdensome; thus Paul says, **which all perish as they are used**, because after the passion of Christ they were deadly to all those who placed their hope in them; but after grace had been spread among the people, such things were deadly to all, absolutely. (I am saying this because it is the opinion of Jerome and Augustine, which I mentioned in commenting on the second chapter of Galatians.) And so they lead to destruction and death.

Why, then, do we still read the Old Testament? I answer that we read it as a witness, but not as something to be observed. Thus Paul says, **which all perish as they are used**, that is, if they are not regarded merely as a witness, but are observed.

133   Further, things that are not founded on reason or authority are vain. But these things are not founded on divine authority, but on human authority. Thus Paul says, **according to human precepts**. But these precepts were from God, were they not? I say that they were, but were to be only for a time, until the truth should come: "For the sake of your tradition you have made void the word of God" (MT 15:6).

Furthermore, they are not founded on reason, because they **have indeed an appearance of wisdom [in superstition]**, meaning, they are based on reasons that lead to superstition, that is, to a religion that is extreme and past its time. And their reasons lead to **self-abasement**, which is not genuine, because a person who has been freed from the slavery of the law by Christ should not submit himself to this slavery again: "Do not submit again to a yoke of slavery" (GAL 5:1). Sometimes precepts that do not rest on divine authority are observed because they are useful for some human purpose.

134 But this is not the case here, for these precepts considered in themselves are a burden. We desire three things: rest, honor and a fulness; and these are not produced by these legal observances. For the ban on foods is opposed to fulness, and becomes a burden because so many rules are involved. Further, these observances do not produce honor, but bring much confusion, as when ashes are sprinkled about and the like: "A yoke upon the disciples which neither our fathers nor we have been able to bear" (AC 15:10). Such practices lead to a **severity to the body**, that is, the Church, and not to the honor of God; rather they **serve only to indulge the flesh**, that is, to satisfy carnal desire.

Chapter 3 ▪ Lectura 1

COLOSSIANS 3:1–7

▪

¹**I**F then you have been raised with Christ, seek the things that are above, where Christ is, seated at the right hand of God. ²**Set your minds on things that are above, not on things that are on earth.** ³**For you have died, and your life is hid with Christ in God.** ⁴**When Christ who is our life appears, then you also will appear with him in glory.** ⁵**Put to death therefore what is earthly in you: immorality, impurity, passion, evil desire, and covetousness, which is idolatry.** ⁶**On account of these the wrath of God is coming [upon the children of despair].** ⁷**In these you once walked, when you lived in them.**

▪

135 Above, the Apostle warned the faithful about those who wished to deceive them; here he teaches them to avoid evil habits. First, he gives his teaching in a general way; second, he presents it in more detail (V. 18). In regard to the first he does two things. First, he teaches them to have a right intention in regard to their end, and in the second place, he instructs them about the rectitude of their human actions (V. 5). The first is divided into two parts. First, he gives the main idea of his teaching, **seek the things that are above**; and second, he gives the reason why they should do so, **for you have died**. In regard to the first he does two things. First, he mentions the benefit they have received; second, he draws his conclusion, **set your minds on things that are above**.

136 The benefit that we have received is that, with the resurrection of Christ, we also have risen. And we have risen in two ways. First, by a hope for our bodily resurrection: "Now if Christ is preached as raised from the dead, how can some of you say that there is no resurrection of the dead?" (1 COR 15:12). In the second way, with the resurrection of Christ we are restored to the life of justice: "He was put to death for our trespasses and raised for our justification" (ROM 4:25). Paul is saying, in effect when Christ arose, you also arose: "He who raised the Lord Jesus will raise us also with Jesus," as we read in 2 Corinthians (4:14).

137 Then when he says, **set your minds on things that are above**, he draws his conclusion about the end: first, that a person should aim at some principal end; and second, that he should judge other things in the light of that end.

138 Paul says, therefore, **If then you have been raised with Christ, seek the things that are above**: "Seek first his kingdom and his righteousness, and all these things shall be yours as well" (MT 6:33). For this is our end: "One thing have I asked of the Lord, that will I seek after; that I may dwell in the house of the Lord all the days of my life" (PS 27:4). Therefore, seek this, **where Christ is, seated at the right hand of God**: "So then the Lord Jesus, after he had spoken to them, was taken up into heaven, and sat down at the right hand of God" (MK 16:19); "Sit at my right hand" (PS 110:1).

By "the right hand of God" he does not mean a member of a body, but he is speaking figuratively, for the right hand of a person is the stronger. Christ sits at the right hand of the Father because, as man, he shares in the stronger and better goods of the Father, while as God, Christ is equal to the Father. Consequently, you should have this intention: that just as Christ died and arose, and was taken up to sit at the right hand of God, so you should die to sin in order to live a life of justice and so be taken up into glory. Or, we could say, that we arose through Christ; but he is seated at the right hand of God, and so our desire should be to be with him: "Wherever the body is, there the eagles will be gathered together" (MT 24:28); "Where your treasure is, there will your heart be also" (MT 6:21).

139 Furthermore, we should judge of other things in the light of Christ; and so Paul says, set **your mind on things that are above, not on things that are on earth**. Here he is affirming one way of life, and rejecting another. A person sets his mind on things that are above, when he governs his life according to heavenly ideas, and judges all things by such ideas: "The wisdom from above" (JAS 3:17). And a person sets his mind on things that are on earth when he orders and judges all things according to earthly goods, considering them the highest goods: "They glory in their shame, with minds set on earthly things" (PHIL 3:19).

140 When Paul continues, **for you have died**, he gives the reason for his advice. First, he mentions their death; second, their hidden life (V. 3b); and third, he teaches when this life will be revealed (V. 4).

141 Just before, Paul had rejected one way of life and affirmed another. Now he returns to these two ways. As to the first he says: Do not set your minds on earthly things, because you have died to an earthly way of life. And a person who has died to this kind of life does not set his mind on the things of this world. This is the way you should act if you have died, with Christ, to the elements of this world: "So you also must consider yourselves dead to sin and alive to God in Christ Jesus" (ROM 6:11); "They are dead, they will not live" (IS 26:14). When he said [above, in Romans], "consider yourselves dead," he followed this with, "and alive."

142   And so there is another life that is hidden. And thus Paul also says here, **and your life is hid with Christ in God**. We acquire this life through Christ. "For Christ also died for sins once for all, the righteous for the unrighteous, that he might bring us to God" (1 PET 3:18). But because this life is obtained through Christ, and Christ is hidden from us because he is in the glory of the Father, this life which is given to us through him is also hidden, namely, where Christ is, in the glory of the Father: "Long life is in his right hand; in his left hand are riches and honor" (PROV 3:16); "O how abundant is your goodness, which you have laid up for those who fear you" (PS 31:19); "To him who conquers I will give some of the hidden manna" (REV 2:17).

143   When he says, **when Christ who is our life appears, then you also will appear with him in glory**, he shows how this life will be manifested, that is, just as Christ's; for we read, "Our God comes" (PS 50:3). And so Paul says, **when Christ who is our life appears**, because he is the Author of our life, and because our life consists in knowing and loving him: "It is no longer I who live, but Christ who lives in me" (GAL 2:20). When Christ appears **then you also will appear**: "When he appears we shall be like him" (1 JN 3:2), that is, in glory: "God came from Teman, and the Holy One from Mount Paran" (HAB 3:3).

144   Next (V. 5) Paul puts order into their actions: first, by restraining them from sin; second, by teaching them about good habits (V. 12). In regard to the first he does two things: First, he starts with a warning; second, he explains it (V. 9b). The first is divided into two parts: First, he forbids carnal vices; second, he gives his reason (V. 6). With respect to the first he does two things: First, he lays down a general prohibition; second, he goes into detail about it (V. 5).

145   He says, **put to death therefore [your members that are on earth]**: You ought not to set your minds on **things that are on earth**, but put to death whatever is earthly, and in particular, **your members that are on earth**. We can explain this by making a comparison: Our life involves many actions, just as our body contains many members. In a good life, prudence is like the eye, which directs a person, and courage is like the feet, which support and carry him. But in an evil life, craftiness becomes the eye, and obstinacy becomes the feet. Therefore, these members must be put to death.

Or we could say that in reference to the members of the body, he had said, "you have died" (v. 3), that is, to an earthly way of life. But how is this death accomplished? He answers, **put to death your members**. Thus, to the extent we have died to sin, to that extent we are alive with grace. For the life of grace heals us with respect to our mind; but not entirely as to our body, because it retains a tendency to sin: "I of myself serve the law of God with my mind, but with my flesh I serve the law of sin" (ROM 7:25); and he said, a little before this: "I see in my members another law at war with the law of my mind and making me captive to the law of sin which dwells in my members" (v. 23). Therefore, because you have died so far as concerns your mind, **put to death** the sinful desires in **your members that are on earth**, insofar as they are on earth and are earthly bodies: "I pommel my body and subdue it" (1 COR 9:27), by not allowing it to be drawn to carnal things.

146   Now he mentions particular sins: first, those that are purely carnal; second, those that are partly carnal. Among the carnal sins, we are inclined to lust especially by concupiscence. Lustful actions are shameful and although they may accord with the nature of man as animal, they are not fitting to it as rational because every sin is opposed to reason. And so Paul says, **immorality**: "Beware, my son, of all immorality" (JOB 4:12). Or, a sin can be against nature, and so he says, **impurity**. Again, pleasure might be impure, and so he says, **passion**; and desire can be depraved, and so he says, **evil desire**.

Second, he lists the intermediate sins. The first of these is **covetousness**, whose object is something corporeal, that is, money, but it is completed in a spiritual delight, that is, in the ownership of such. And thus it has some part among the carnal sins. Paul adds, **which is idolatry**: "one who is covetous that is, an idolater," as Ephesians (5:5) says.

147   But is covetousness by its nature really a kind of idolatry, and does a covetous person sin as an idolater sins? I say, not specifically, but by resemblance, because a covetous person puts his very life in money. We have idolatry when someone gives to some image the honor owed to God; but a covetous person gives to money the honor owed to God, because he builds his whole life around it. But because a covetous person intends to act toward money as to God, like an idolater, it is a lesser sin.

148   Then when Paul says, **on account of these the wrath of God is coming**, he gives the reason why these sins should be avoided. There are two reasons: The first applies to all; the second applies especially to them. The first is God's punishment, because on account of carnal sins **the wrath of God**, that is, God's punishment, **is coming [upon the children of despair]**, that is, sinners. Such sinners despair of God because lust is the offspring of despair, since many people abandon themselves entirely to things of the flesh because they have despaired of spiritual things. Or, he says **children of despair**, because of themselves there is no hope for their correction. And so the wrath of God is coming, as in the flood (GEN 6, 7), and on the people of Sodom.

The other reason they have for avoiding these sins is that once they did live that way; and so Paul says, **in these you once walked**, from bad to worse. He gives them this reason, first, because of what Peter says: "Let the time that is past suffice for doing what the Gentiles like to do, living in licentiousness, passions, drunkenness, revels, carousing, and lawless idolatry" (1 PET 4:3). Second, he mentions this reason because they knew from their own experience that such conduct is not beneficial, but only brings disorder: "But then what return did you get from the things of which you are now ashamed," as we read in Romans (6:21).

Chapter 3 ▪ Lectura 2

COLOSSIANS 3:8–11

▪
---

⁸**BUT** now put them all away: anger, wrath, malice, slander, and foul talk from your mouth. ⁹Do not lie to one another, seeing that you have put off the old nature with its practices ¹⁰and have put on the new nature, which is being renewed in knowledge after the image of its creator. ¹¹Here there cannot be Greek and Jew, circumcised and uncircumcised, barbarian, Scythian, slave, free man, but Christ is all, and in all.

▪
---

149   Above, the Apostle warned the faithful about sins of the flesh; here he warns them about spiritual sins. First, he lays down a general admonition; and second, he divides it into parts.

150   So he says: At one time you walked in sins, **but now put them all away**, not only sins of the flesh, but all sin: "So put away all malice and all guile and insincerity and envy and all slander" (1 PET 2:1).

151   He divides the spiritual sins into two groups: first, into sins of the heart; second, into sins of the mouth, spoken sins. First of all, he mentions **anger**: "For the anger of man does not work the righteousness of God" (JAS 1:20) and this must be avoided. Second, he mentions **wrath**, which springs from anger, and occurs when a person considers someone unworthy of what he has, or in comparison with another: "I have no wrath" (IS 27:4). **Malice** then follows after these two, when a person tries to cause injury to his neighbor: "Put away all filthiness and rank growth of wickedness" (JAS 1:21).

152   Then he mentions those sins committed by word; and there are three kinds. Such sins indicate a spiritual disorder. First, such a sin in relation to God is **[blasphemy]**: "Bring out of the camp him who blasphemed; and let all who hear him lay their hands upon his head, and let all the congregation stone him" (LEV 24:14). And thus all blasphemy is a grievous sin. But what if it is sudden? I answer that if it is so sudden that a person does not realize that he is blaspheming, it is not a grievous sin. But I believe that however suddenly, if a person realizes that he is speaking blasphemous words, he sins in a grievous way.

Second, he mentions a disorder concerning concupiscence, when he says, **put foul talk from your mouth**: "Let no evil talk come out of your mouths" (EPH 4:29). Third, he mentions a disorder in relation to our neighbor, lying: "A false witness will not go unpunished" (PROV 19:5).

153   Then when he says, **seeing that you have put off the old nature**, he shows why the vices he has just mentioned must be avoided, the reason being that when one puts off what is old, he should put on what is new: "No one sews an old patch on a new garment," as we read in Matthew (9:16). First, he talks of putting off what is old, second, of putting on what is new (V. 10).

154   So Paul tells us to get rid of these things, **put off the old nature**, because it has grown old by sin: "What is becoming obsolete and growing old is ready to vanish away" (HEB 8:13). This old nature, this old self, is approaching decay, because sin is the road to decay. In addition, sin destroys virtue and spiritual beauty. The oldness of our nature, of course, was brought in by the sin of our first parent: "Therefore as sin came into the world through one man and death through sin, and so death spread to all men because all men sinned" (ROM 5:12). This old nature, therefore, or old self, is the oldness of sin: "We know that our old self was crucified with him so that the sinful body might be destroyed" (ROM 6:6). We are to put off this old self **with its practices**: "Put off your old nature which belongs to your former manner of life and is corrupt through deceitful lusts" (EPH 4:22).

The new nature or self is the mind, renewed from within, because before grace our mind is subject within to sin, and when it is renewed by grace it becomes new: "Your youth is renewed like the eagle's" (PS 103:5); "For neither circumcision counts for anything, nor uncircumcision, but a new creation" (GAL 6:15). This new creation is renewing grace. Yet, there is an oldness that still remains in our flesh. Nevertheless, if you follow the judgment of the new nature, the new self, you are putting on the new nature or new self; while if you lust according to the desires of the flesh, you are putting on the old self or nature: "Put on the new nature, created after the likeness of God in true righteousness and holiness" (EPH 4:24).

155 Then when Paul says, **and have put on the new nature**, he describes the new self. First, he shows how this renewal takes place; second, where it takes place.

He shows that the inner self, having become old by its ignorance of God, is made new by faith and the knowledge of God: "We are being changed into his likeness from one degree of glory to another" (2 COR 3:18). And where is this renewal taking place? It is taking place where the image of God is, and this is not in the sense faculties, but in the mind. And so Paul says, **after** [in the sense of "with respect to"] **the image of its creator**. In other words, the image of God in us is being renewed.

156 Then (V. 11) he shows that this renewal is for every one, otherwise it would not pertain to human nature as such. And this renewal pertains to all because it was accomplished with respect to what is common to all. Here then we have five ways in which people are different. The first way is by sex, which Paul excludes when he says, **here there cannot be [male and female]**, because men and women do not differ in mind, but in their physical sex. Second, people are made different by their native lands, and Paul excludes this when he says, **Greek and Jew**. For although the Jews were believers and the Greeks unbelievers, yet both have rational minds: "Or is God the God of Jews only? Is he not the God of Gentiles also?" (ROM 3:29). The third distinction is based on rite [as the rite of circumcision], for some had the law, while others did not; yet "the same Lord is Lord of all and bestows his riches upon all who call upon Him," as Romans (10:12) says. A fourth difference is in language: **barbarian, Scythian**. Scythia is toward the north. What is barbarous is what is foreign or alien. Thus barbarians are foreigners, and one is absolutely a barbarian who is alien to human nature as such, that is, insofar as it is rational. And so barbarians are those people who are not ruled by reason and laws; they are slaves by nature. But there is no difference in Christ, because although they do not have the civil law, they still have the law of Christ. The final difference is based on state: for some are **slave**, and others **free**; but in Christ they are all alike: "The small and the great are there, and the slave is free from his master" (JOB 3:19).

Therefore, none of these differences exist in Christ, **but Christ is all, and in all**. For circumcision is obtained through Christ alone, and freedom comes from Christ alone. If you are not free, Christ is your freedom; if you are not circumcised, Christ is your circumcision; and so on. And Christ is in all, because he gives his gifts to all.

Chapter 3 ▪ Lectura 3

COLOSSIANS 3:12–17

▪

¹²PUT on then, as God's chosen ones, holy and beloved, compassion, kindness, lowliness, meekness, and patience, ¹³forbearing one another and, if one has a complaint against another, forgiving each other; as the Lord has forgiven you, so you also must forgive. ¹⁴And above all these put on love, which binds everything together in perfect harmony. ¹⁵And let the peace of Christ rule in your hearts, to which indeed you were called in the one body. And be thankful. ¹⁶Let the word of Christ dwell in you richly, as you teach and admonish one another in all wisdom, and as you sing psalms, and hymns and spiritual songs with thankfulness in your hearts to God. ¹⁷And whatever you do, in word or deed, do everything in the name of the Lord Jesus, giving thanks to God the Father through him.

▪

157 Above, the Apostle urged the faithful to avoid evil, and here he urges them to accomplish what is good: first, he urges the acts of the particular virtues, and second, the acts of those principal virtues that perfect the others (V. 14). First, he reminds them of their present condition; second, he gives a list of the virtues (V. 12b).

158   Paul says: If you have put on the new self, you should put on the parts of the new self, that is, the virtues: "Let us then cast off the works of darkness and put on the armor of light" (ROM 13:12). We put these on when our exterior actions are made pleasing by the virtues.

But which virtues? Some things are appropriate for soldiers, other things for priests. **Put on then** what is appropriate for yourself, **as God's chosen ones, holy and beloved**. When he says chosen, this refers to the taking away of evil; and holy, refers to the gift of grace. "But you were washed, you were sanctified" (1 COR 6:11); "You shall be holy; for I the Lord your God am holy" (LEV 19:2). When he says **beloved**, he is referring to their preparation for future glory: "He loved them to the end," that is, of eternal life (JN 13:1).

159   Then, he describes what we are to put on which will protect us in good times and in bad times: "With the weapons of righteousness for the right hand and for the left" (2 COR 6:7). First, he mentions what we must have in prosperity, and second, in times of adversity.

160   When times are good we owe compassion or mercy to our neighbor; and so Paul says, **compassion**: "Through the tender mercy of our God, when the day shall dawn upon us from on high" (LK 1:78); "If there is any affection and sympathy" (PHIL 3:1), that is, compassion springing from love. Second, we must show **kindness** to all. Kindness *[benignitas]* is like a good fire *[bona igneitas]*. For fire melts and thaws what is moist, and if there is a good fire in you it will melt and thaw what is moist. It is the Holy Spirit who does this: "The Spirit of wisdom is kind" (WIS 1:6); "Be kind to one another" (EPH 4:32). Lowliness or humility should be found in your hearts: "The greater you are, the more you must humble yourself" (SIR 3:18). In external matters you should practice **[moderation]**, which consists in a certain limit, so that you do not go to extremes in times of prosperity: "Let all men know of your moderation," as Philippians (4:5) says.

161 In the bad times of adversity three kinds of armor are necessary. First, patience, which keeps the soul from giving up the love of God and what is right because of difficulties: "You will save your souls by patience" (LK 21:19). Sometimes it happens that a person does what is right if he alone is involved, yet he finds that the traits of other persons are insufferable; and to these he says, **forbearing one another**: "For by what that righteous man saw and heard as he lived among them, he was vexed in his righteous soul day after day with their lawless deeds" (2 PET 2:8); "We who are strong ought to bear with the failings of the weak, and not to please ourselves," as we read in Romans (15:1).

Third, the armor of pardon is necessary, and so he says, **forgiving each other**: "What I have forgiven, if I have forgiven anything, has been for your sake in the presence of Christ" (2 COR 2:10). One forgives an injury when he does not hold a grudge against the person who did it to him, and does not injure him in return. Still, when punishment is necessary, the person committing the injury must be punished. Paul adds the reason why they should forgive **as the Lord has forgiven you**: "Does a man harbor anger against another, and yet seek for healing from the Lord?" (SIR 28:3); "I forgave you all that debt because you besought me" (MT 18:32), and then he continues, "and should not you have had mercy on your fellow servant, as I had mercy on you?"

162 Then when Paul says, **and above all these put on love**, he urges them to practice the principal virtues, which perfect the others. Among the virtues, the love of charity holds first place; while among the gifts, wisdom is first. For love is the soul of all the virtues, while wisdom directs them. First, he leads them to the practice of love, and second to wisdom (V. 16). First, he urges them to possess the love of charity; second, to possess the effects of this love (V. 15).

163 So Paul says, **above all these put on love**, which is greater than all the virtues mentioned above, as we find stated in 1 Corinthians (13:13). **Above all these**, that is, more than all the others, because love is the end of all the virtues: "The end of the commandment is love" (1 TIM 1:5). Or we could say, above all these we should have love, because it is above all the rest: "I will show you a still more excellent way" (1 COR 12:31). Love is above all the rest because without it the others are of no value. This love is the seamless tunic mentioned by John (19:23).

The reason we need this love is because it **binds everything together in perfect harmony**. According to the Gloss, all the virtues perfect man, but love unites them to each other and makes them permanent; and this is why it is said to bind. Or, it is said to bind because it binds of its very nature, for love unites the beloved to the lover: "I led them with cords of compassion, with the bands of love" (HOS 11:4). He says, **perfect**, because a thing is perfect when it holds firmly to its ultimate end; and love does this.

164 Then (V. 15), he urges them to acts of love. He mentions two of these acts, peace and thankfulness, and implies a third, joy. He says, **let the peace of Christ [rejoice] in your hearts**. An immediate effect of the love of charity is peace, which is, as Augustine comments, that composure or calmness of order produced in a person by God. Love does this, because when one loves another he harmonizes his will with the other: "Great peace have those who love thy law" (PS 119:165).

He says **rejoice**, because the effect of this love is joy, and this joy follows peace: "Joy follows those who take counsels of peace" (PROV 12:20). Paul does not merely say "peace," because there is a peace of this world that God did not come to bring. He says, **the**

peace of Christ, the peace Christ established between God and man. Jesus affirmed this peace: "Jesus himself stood among them and said to them: Peace to you" (LK 24:36). And you should have this peace, because it is **the peace . . . to which indeed you were called**. "God has called us to peace" (1 COR 7:15). He adds, **in the one body**, that is, that you may be in one body. Another effect is thankfulness, and so Paul continues, **and be thankful**: "The hope of the unthankful will melt away like the winter's ice" (WIS 16:29).

165 Next (V. 16) he urges them to acquire wisdom: First, he teaches them about the source of wisdom, and second its usefulness.

166 In order to have true wisdom, one must inquire into its source, and so Paul says, **let the word of Christ dwell in you richly**. "The source of wisdom is God's word in the highest heaven" (SIR 1:5). Therefore you should draw wisdom from the word of Christ: "That will be your wisdom and your understanding in the sight of the peoples" (DEUT 4:6); "He was made our wisdom" (1 COR 1:30). But some people do not have the Word, and so they do not have wisdom. He says that this wisdom should **dwell** in us: "Bind them about your neck, write them on the tablet of your heart" (PROV 3:3).

For some, a little of Christ's word is enough, but the Apostle wants them to have much more; thus he says, **let the word of God dwell in you richly**: "God is able to provide you with every blessing in abundance, so that you may always have enough of everything" (2 COR 9:8); "Search for it as for hidden treasures" (PROV 2:4). He adds, **in all wisdom**, that is, you should want to know everything that pertains to the wisdom of Christ: "I did not shrink from declaring to you the whole counsel of God" (ACTS 20:27); "The heart of a fool is like a broken jar; it will hold no wisdom" (SIR 21:17) [Vulgate].

167 This wisdom is useful in three ways: for instruction, for devotion, and for direction.

168 It instructs us in two ways: first, to know what is true; and so Paul says, **as you teach**. He is saying, in effect: This wisdom dwells in you so richly that it can teach you all things: "All scripture is inspired by God and profitable for teaching, for reproof, for correction, and for training in righteousness" (2 TIM 3:16). Second, this wisdom instructs us to know what is good, and so Paul says, **and admonish one another**, that is, encourage yourselves to do good things: "To arouse you by way of reminder" (2 PET 1:1).

169 Second, he mentions its usefulness for devotion, saying, **as you sing psalms and hymns**. The psalms show the delight of acting well: "Praise him with joy" (PS 148:2/47:1). A hymn is a song of praise: "A hymn for all his saints" (PS 148:14).

And spiritual songs with thankfulness in your hearts to God, because whatever we do, we should relate it to spiritual goods, to the eternal promises, and to the worship of God. And so Paul says, **in your hearts**, not only with your lips: "I will pray with the spirit and I will pray with the mind also" (1 COR 14:15); "This people draws near with their mouth and honors me with their lips, while their hearts are far from me" (IS 29:13). He adds, **with thankfulness**, that is, acknowledging the grace of Christ and God's gifts. The chief songs of the Church are songs of the heart; but they are expressed vocally so as to arouse the songs of the heart, and for the benefit of the simple and uncultured.

170 He mentions the usefulness of this wisdom in directing our actions when he says, **and whatever you do, in word or deed, do everything in the name of the Lord Jesus Christ**, because even our speaking is a work: "Whether your eat or drink, or whatever you do, do all to the glory of God" (1 COR 10:31).

Some find a difficulty in this statement of Paul: for what he is saying is either a command or a counsel. If it is a command, then whoever does not do this sins; yet a person sins venially when he does not do this; therefore, whoever sins venially sins mortally.

My answer is this: Some say that this is a counsel; but this is not true. Nevertheless, it is not necessary that we refer everything to God in an actual way; it can be done habitually. Whoever acts against the glory of God and his commands, acts against this command. But one who sins venially does not act against this command in an absolute way, because even though he does not refer everything to God in an actual way, he does so habitually.

Chapter 3 ▪ Lectura 4

COLOSSIANS 3:18–25; 4:1

---

¹⁸**WIVES, be subject to your husbands, as is fitting in the Lord. ¹⁹Husbands, love your wives, and do not be harsh with them. ²⁰Children, obey your parents in everything, for this pleases the Lord. ²¹Fathers, do not provoke your children, lest they become discouraged. ²²Slaves, obey in everything those who are your earthly masters, not with eyeservice, as men-pleasers, but in singleness of heart, fearing the Lord. ²³Whatever your task, work heartily, as serving the Lord and not men, ²⁴knowing that from the Lord you will receive the inheritance as your reward; you are serving the Lord Christ. ²⁵For the wrong-doer will be paid back for the wrong he has done, and there is no partiality.**

¹Masters, treat your slaves justly and fairly, knowing that you also have a Master in heaven.

---

171   Having given a general direction to all, Paul now begins to give particular directions. First, he gives special directions that relate to the various states found in the Church; second, certain directions that apply to all states in certain conditions (4:2). There are three special directions, according to the three kinds of relationships the Philosopher finds in domestic society: that of husband and wife; father and child; and master and slave (v. 22).

Each of these is divided into two parts insofar as he urges subjects to obey and their superiors to govern with moderation.

172   He says, **wives, be subject to your husbands**, and adds, **as is fitting**, because this has been decreed by God's law: "You shall be under your husband's power, and he shall have dominion over you" (GEN 3:16); "The women should keep silence in the churches. For they are not permitted to speak, but should be subordinate, as even the law says" (1 COR 14:34). The reason for this is that ruling is a function of reason; and because men's reason is stronger, they should preside. He adds, **in the Lord**, because all things directed to certain ends must ultimately be referred to God.

173   Then, he instructs husbands to love their wives, **husbands, love your wives**; because this is natural, since a husband and wife are in a certain sense one: "Husbands, love your wives, as Christ loved the Church" (EPH 5:25). He forbids them to be bitter: "She who is bitter becomes weak in doing good" (MIC 1:12), "Let all bitterness and wrath and anger and clamor and slander be put away from you, with all malice" (EPH 4:31).

174   Then he deals with the second relationship, and says, **children, obey your parents in everything**, that is, everything that is not contrary to God: "We have had earthly fathers to discipline us and we respected them" (HEB 12:9). But if they command anything that is contrary to God, then we must remember what is said in Luke: "If any one comes to me and does not hate his own father and mother and wife and children and brothers and sisters, yes, and even his own life, he cannot be my disciple" (14:26). This is to be done **for this pleases the Lord**, that is, it is in the Lord's law, because the law of charity does not destroy the law of nature, but perfects it. And it is a natural law that a child is subject to the care of his father: "Honor your father and your mother" (EX 20:12).

175 Then when Paul says, **fathers, do not provoke your children**, he instructs parents: "Fathers, do not provoke your children to anger" (EPH 6:4). They should not do this **lest they become discouraged**, that is, fainthearted. Paul gives this advice because adults keep the impressions they have had as children. And it is natural for those raised in slavery to be always fainthearted. This is why some say that the children of Israel were not immediately led into the promised land: they had been raised in slavery, and would not have had the courage to fight against their enemies: "Say to those who are of a fearful heart: Be strong, fear not!" (IS 35:4).

176 Next, he considers the third relationship. First, he instructs the slaves; second, he gives the reason for what he says (V. 24); and third, he clears up a question (V. 25). As to the first, he does two things: first, he tells them to obey; and second, how to obey.

177 He says, slaves, according to your state in this world, obey in everything, that is, in everything that is not against God, **those who are your earthly masters**: "Not only to the kind and gentle but also to the overbearing" (1 PET 2:18); "Let all who are under the yoke of slavery regard their masters as worthy of all honor" (1 TIM 6:1).

178 Then when he says, **not with eyeservice**, he teaches them how they are to obey. He shows them two ways to obey: first, with simplicity and without trickery; second, willingly.

So Paul says, **not with eyeservice**, that is, not merely to the extent that they can be seen by their master. This same idea is found in Ephesians (6:6). He says, **not as men-pleasers**, for such persons serve merely to please men. As Galatians says (1:10): "If I were still pleasing men, I should not be a servant of Christ." And therefore he adds, **but in singleness of heart**, that is, without trickery, **fearing the Lord**, as in Job (1:1): "That man was simple and upright, and feared God"; "The simplicity of the upright guides them" (PROV 11:3).

Further, they should serve willingly; and so Paul says, **whatever your task, work heartily**, that is, readily. And they are to do this **as serving the Lord**, because one who serves another because it is the right thing to do does this because of God, the source of what is right: "He who resists the authorities resists what God has appointed" (ROM 13:2); "Doing the will of God from the heart, rendering service with a good will as to the Lord and not to men" (EPH 6:6).

179 Next, he gives two reasons why they should serve this way. The first considers their reward, and the second considers their devotion to God. So Paul says: Serve readily, because **from the Lord you will receive the eternal inheritance as your reward**: "The lines have fallen for me in pleasant places; yea, I have a goodly heritage" (PS 16:6); "Knowing that whatever good any one does, he will receive the same again from the Lord, whether he is a slave or free" (EPH 6:8).

Some people were of the opinion that it is not meritorious to accomplish an act of justice, because this seems to be owed to someone, and it is not meritorious to give to someone what is his due. But we should remember that by the very fact that we do this voluntarily, we are doing something of ourselves, because it is in our power to will or not to will; and so such an act is meritorious. Now slaves serve their masters because they owe this to them; and therefore, in order to receive their reward, they should do this voluntarily. But they should serve their masters in such a way that they do not separate themselves from God. The second reason for serving this way is that this is the way one serves the Lord; as we read in Romans (12:11): "Be aglow with the Spirit, serve the Lord."

180 Then (V. 25) he clears up a question. For a slave might ask: How can I serve a person who harms me? And so Paul replies. It is not up to you to take revenge by taking away from him what is his; rather, wait for the one who can, **for the wrong-doer will be paid back for the wrong he has done**: "For we must all appear before the judgment seat of Christ, so that each one may receive good or evil, according to what he has done in the body" (2 COR 5:10); "There is no partiality with him [God]" (EPH 6:9); and also in Acts (10:34): "God shows no partiality."

181   Next, Paul shows how masters should treat their slaves. He does two things: First, he gives his instructions, second, the reason for them. There are two ways a master can oppress his slaves. First, by acting unjustly against them by violating the laws, for according to the laws a master cannot be cruel to his slaves. And so Paul says that masters should treat their slaves justly. Second, by demanding that their slaves accomplish absolutely all their duties, which a Christian gentleness would soften; and so Paul says, **fairly**: "If I have rejected the cause of my manservant or my maidservant, when they brought a complaint against me; what then shall I do when God rises up?" as we read in Job (31:13).

Then when he says, **knowing that you also have a Master in heaven**, Paul gives the reason why they should act this way, and it is this: Just as you act toward your slaves, so the Lord will act toward you: "Knowing that he who is both their Master and yours is in heaven" (EPH 6:9).

Chapter 4 ▪ Lectura 1

COLOSSIANS 4:2–18

---

²CONTINUE steadfastly in prayer, being watchful in it with thanksgiving; ³and pray for us also, that God may open to us a door for the word, to declare the mystery of Christ, on account of which I am in prison, ⁴that I may make it clear, as I ought to speak. ⁵Conduct yourselves wisely toward outsiders, making the most of the time. ⁶Let your speech always be gracious, seasoned with salt, so that you may know how you ought to answer every one. ⁷Tychicus will tell you all about my affairs; he is a beloved brother and faithful minister and fellow servant in the Lord. ⁸I have sent him to you for this very purpose, that you may know how we are and that he may encourage your hearts, ⁹and with him Onesimus, the faithful and beloved brother, who is one of yourselves. They will tell you of every thing that has taken place here. ¹⁰Aristarchus my fellow prisoner greets you, and Mark the cousin of Barnabas (concerning whom you have received instructions—if he comes to you, receive him), ¹¹and Jesus who is called Justus. These are the only men of the circumcision among my fellow workers for the kingdom of God, and they have been a comfort to me. ¹²Epaphras, who is one of yourselves, a servant of Christ Jesus, greets you, always remembering you earnestly in his prayers, that you may stand

mature and fully assured in all the will of God. ¹³For I bear him witness that he has worked hard for you and for those in Laodicea and in Hierapolis. ¹⁴Luke the beloved physician and Demas greet you. ¹⁵Give my greetings to the brethren at Laodicea, and to Nympha and the church in her house. ¹⁶And when this letter has been read among you, have it read also in the church of the Laodiceans; and see that you read also the letter from Laodicea. ¹⁷And say to Archippus, "See that you fulfil the ministry which you have received in the Lord." ¹⁸I, Paul, write this greeting with my own hand. Remember my fetters. Grace be with you.

---

182   Above, Paul gave specific teachings for each class of persons; here he gives instructions to everyone. First, he shows what their relationship to others ought to be; and second, how some will be acting toward them (V. 7). In regard to the first he does two things: First, he shows how they should act toward him, the Apostle, their prelate; and second, toward others, especially, unbelievers (V. 5). In regard to the first he does two things: First, he urges them to pray in general; second, to pray for him (V. 3).

183   Prayer should have three characteristics: It should be constant, alert, and with gratitude. It should be constant, and so Paul says, **continue steadfastly in prayer**, that is, pray with perseverance: "Pray constantly" (1 TH 5:17); "They ought always to pray and not lose heart" (LK 18:1). It should also be alert, so that the mind does not become oppressed; and so Paul adds, **being watchful**: "Watch with your prayers" (1 PET 4:7); and in Luke we read: "All night he continued in prayer to God" (LK 6:12). Prayer should also be with gratitude, that is, with thanksgiving; for if we are ungrateful for the good things we have received, we do not deserve new favors.

And so Paul continues, **with thanksgiving**: "Give thanks in all circumstances" (1 TH 5:18); and in Philippians (4:6) we have "but in everything by prayer and supplication with thanksgiving."

184   Next, Paul asks them to pray for him, saying, **and pray for us also,** because subjects should pray for their prelates; for their prelates watch over them, and the welfare of the prelates affects all of their subjects: "Pray for us, that the word of the Lord may speed on and triumph" (2 TH 3:1). They should pray **that God may open to us a door for the word**, that is, the door of our mouth, through which the words coming from our heart pass; and they should pray that God give to Paul the grace to preach his word in a fitting manner. This opening also points to something great: "And he opened his mouth and taught them" (MT 5:2); and so Paul adds, **to declare the mystery of Christ**: "He utters mysteries in the Spirit" (1 COR 14:2). And I, Paul, need these things, because I am suffering for the word of Christ. And so you must pray that I can do so boldly: "The gospel for which I am suffering and wearing fetters like a criminal" (2 TIM 2:9). You must pray that God **may open**, that is, unblock, **to us a door for the word**.

185   There are three obstacles that can block the word. One is fear, and so Paul says, **I am in prison.** The second is its profundity, so that it cannot be understood by the faithful; and so Paul says, **that I may make it clear.** The third obstacle is that the way it is preached or the time may not be appropriate; and so Paul says, **as I ought to speak**. "But I brethren, could not address you as spiritual men, but as men of the flesh" (1 COR 3:1); "Who then is the faithful and wise steward whom his master will set over his household, to give them their portion of food at the proper time?" (LK 12:42).

186   Then (V. 5) he shows how they should act toward outsiders: first, as to their manner of life; second, in what they say (V. 6).

187 Paul says, **conduct yourselves wisely toward outsiders**, that is, unbelievers. And do so wisely, with wisdom: "For God loves nothing so much as the man who lives with wisdom" (WIS 7:28). The reason for doing this is that they may be **making the most of the time**. A person makes the most of his trouble when he overlooks what is owing to him, in order to avoid trouble. Now, they were being troubled by these outsiders. And so Paul wants them to make the most of this trouble by means of wisdom: "Maintain good conduct among the Gentiles" (1 PET 2:12).

188 Paul also instructs them as to their speech. First, it should be gracious; and so he says, **let your speech always be gracious**; "A gracious tongue multiplies courtesies" (SIR 6:5). Second, it should be considerate; and so he says, **seasoned with salt**. Salt signifies considerateness or discretion, because just as salt makes food savory, so every inconsiderate action is bitter and irregular: "Have salt in yourselves, and be at peace with one another" (MK 9:50). They should do these things **so that you may know how you ought to answer every one**. For those who have wisdom should be answered one way; and the foolish are to be answered in another way: "Answer not a fool according to his folly, lest you be like him yourself" (PROV 26:4); "Always be prepared to make a defense to any one who calls you to account for the hope that is in you," as we read in 1 Peter (3:15).

189 Next, Paul tells them about some others. First, about those whom he is sending to them; and second, about those who are staying with him (V. 10).

190 Paul is sending to them a representative, whom he now describes in three ways. First, as to love, saying, a **beloved brother**, that is, by the love of charity, which makes a person more precious than gold: "A man will be more precious than gold" (Is 13:12). Second, he is described as to his faith, a **faithful minister**: "It is required of stewards that they be found trustworthy" (1 COR 4:2). Third, from his humility; and so Paul says, **fellow servant**, in the ministry, but a fellow servant **in the Lord**, because a prelate should be looking out for the honor of God and for the benefit of those over whom he has charge.

Why is Tychicus being sent? To learn the condition of the faithful. "Go now, see if it is well with your brothers, and with the flock; and bring me word again" (GEN 37:14); "See how your brothers fare, and bring some token from them" (1 SAM 17:18). He is also to encourage and comfort them: "For I long to see you, that I may impart to you some spiritual gift to strengthen you, that is, that we may be mutually encouraged by each other's faith" (ROM 1:11). Our Lord, who was sent by the Father, also came for this purpose: "to comfort all who mourn" (Is 61:2).

Then he mentions his companion, **and with him Onesimus**. These two **will tell you of everything that has taken place here**; they will relate what you are doing to me for correction, and tell you what I am doing so you may have an example.

191   Then when he says, **Aristarchus my fellow prisoner greets you**, he shows how those who are remaining with the Apostle greet them. The text is clear.

And Mark the cousin of Barnabas, concerning whom you have received instructions. We read in Acts (15:37) that a certain person by the name of John, surnamed Mark, had left Paul and Barnabas when they set out on one of their journeys; however, he later returned to them. Barnabas wanted to take him back, but Paul refused. As a result, Paul and Barnabas went their different ways. Later, Paul wrote to the Colossians that they were not to receive Mark. But now, since Mark had changed, he asks them to receive him. Thus, **concerning whom you have received instructions: if he comes to you, receive him**. Or, it could be understood this way: **And Mark the cousin of Barnabas, concerning whom,** that is, Barnabas, **you have received instructions.**

And Jesus who is called Justus; he was a holy man, and so was called "Justus" [the Just]. **These are the only men of the circumcision,** sent to preach the Good News of Christ: "What then? Only that in every way, whether in pretense or in truth, Christ is proclaimed; and in that I rejoice" (PHIL 1:18). Thus he mentions the Gentiles first, and then the Jews. **Epaphras, who is one of yourselves,** because he was an Asian. Their wish for the Colossians is "that you may be perfect and complete, lacking in nothing" (JAS 1:4); **that you may stand mature and fully assured in all the will of God,** that is, in all things relating to the will of God.

Then he mentions Luke, who it seems, was not Jewish by birth, because he was from Antioch, and a physician. He singles him out because he had great authority in the Church because of the Gospel he wrote while the Apostle was still alive. He also mentions **Demas.**

192 Next (V. 15) he mentions those whom the Colossians ought to greet: First, those from another church; and second, those in their own. We can see from what he says, **see that you read also the letter from Laodicea,** that Paul wrote other letters: the one to the Laodiceans mentioned here, and another to the Corinthians, besides the first and second, because in 1 Corinthians (5:9) he says: "I wrote to you in my letter not to associate with immoral men."

There are two reasons why they are not in the canon: either there was some doubt about their authority, because they were possibly distorted, and had been destroyed in the churches, or because they contained nothing different from the others.

193 **And say to Archippus.** He was their prelate, and he tells them to warn him: **See that you fulfil the ministry that you have received in the Lord:** "Fulfil your ministry" (2 TIM 4:5). One is said to fulfil his ministry when he does that for which he received it.

Still, it does not seem proper for those in a congregation to warn their own prelate (EX 19:24). I answer that a member of the congregation is forbidden to rebuke him sharply or insult him, but he can warn him in a charitable way as Paul rebuked Peter (GAL 2:11). But why did he not write to the prelate? Because the prelate exists for the Church and not the Church for the prelate.

194   I, Paul, write this greeting with my own hand. It was the Apostle's practice to have someone else write the entire letter, and at the end of it he would write something in his own hand, as in 2 Thessalonians (3:17): "I, Paul, write this greeting with my own hand." He does the same here, so that they will not be deceived. (And he says, **Remember my fetters**, because he was fettered in Rome): "As an example of suffering and patience, brethren, take the prophets who spoke in the name of the Lord" (JAS 5:10); "Remember your leaders, those who spoke to you the word of God; consider the outcome of their life, and imitate their faith" (HEB 13:7).

Then he wishes them well, concluding: **Grace be with you**: "Grace and truth came through Jesus Christ" (JN 1:17), to Whom be praise and glory now and forever. Amen.